THE

ROMAN QUESTION.

BY

E. ABOUT.

TRANSLATED FROM THE FRENCH,

BY

H. C. COAPE.

NEW YORK:
D. APPLETON AND COMPANY,
346 & 348 BROADWAY.
1859.

PREFACE.

It was in the Papal States that I studied the Roman Question. I travelled over every part of the country; I conversed with men of all opinions, examined things very closely, and collected my information on the spot.

My first impressions, noted down from day to day without any especial object, appeared, with some necessary modifications, in the *Moniteur Universel*. These notes, truthful, somewhat unconnected, and so thoroughly impartial, that it would be easy to discover in them contradictions and inconsistencies, I was obliged to discontinue, in consequence of the violent outcry of the Pontifical Government. I did more. I threw them in the fire, and wrote a book instead. The present volume is the result of a year's reflection.

I completed my study of the subject by the perusal of the most recent works published in Italy. The learned memoir of the Marquis Pepoli, and the admirable reply of an anonymous writer to M. de

Rayneval, supplied me with my best weapons. I have been further enlightened by the conversation and correspondence of some illustrious Italians, whom I would gladly name, were I not afraid of exposing them to danger.

The pressing condition of Italy has obliged me to write more rapidly than I could have wished; and this enforced haste has given a certain air of warmth, perhaps of intemperance, even to the most carefully matured reflections. It was my intention to produce a memoir,—I fear I may be charged with having written a pamphlet. Pardon me certain vivacities of style, which I had not time to correct, and plunge boldly into the heart of the book. You will find something there.

I fight fairly, and in good faith. I do not pretend to have judged the foes of Italy without passion; but I have calumniated none of them.

If I have sought a publisher in Brussels, while I had an excellent one in Paris, it is not because I feel any alarm on the score of the regulations of our press, or the severity of our tribunals. But as the Pope has a long arm, which might reach me in France, I have gone a little out of the way to tell him the plain truths contained in these pages.

May 9, 1859.

CONTENTS.

THE ROMAN QUESTION.

CHAPTER I.

THE POPE AS A KING.

THE Roman Catholic Church, which I sincerely respect, consists of one hundred and thirty-nine millions of individuals —without counting little Mortara.

It is governed by seventy Cardinals, or Princes of the Church, in memory of the twelve Apostles.

The Cardinal-Bishop of Rome, who is also designated by the name of Vicar of Jesus Christ, Holy Father, or Pope, is invested with boundless authority over the minds of these hundred and thirty-nine millions of Catholics.

The Cardinals are nominated by the Pope; the Pope is nominated by the Cardinals; from the day of his election he becomes infallible, at least in the opinion of M. de Maistre, and the best Catholics of our time.

This was not the opinion of Bossuet; but it has always been that of the Popes themselves.

When the Sovereign Pontiff declares to us that the Virgin Mary was born free from original sin, the hundred and thirty-nine millions of Catholics are bound to believe it on his word. This is what has recently occurred.

This discipline of the understanding reflects infinite credit upon the nineteenth century. If posterity does us justice, it will be grateful to us therefor. It will see that instead of cutting one another's throats about theological questions, we have surveyed lines of railway, laid telegraphs, constructed steam-engines, launched ships, pierced isthmuses, created sciences, corrected laws, repressed factions, fed the poor, civilized barbarians, drained marshes, cultivated waste lands, without ever having a single dispute as to the infallibility of a man.

But the busiest age, the age which the best knows the value of time, may be obliged for a moment to neglect its business. If, for instance, it should remark around Rome and its Bishop a violent agitation, which neither the trickery of diplomacy nor the pressure of armies can suppress; if it perceive in a little corner of a peninsula a smouldering fire, which may at any moment burst forth, and in twenty-four hours envelope all Europe, this age, prudent from a sense of duty, on account of the great things it has to accomplish, turns its attention to the situation of Rome, and insists upon knowing what it all means.

It means that the simple princes of the middle ages, Pepin the Brief, Charlemagne, and the Countess Matilda, behaved with great liberality to the Pope. They gave him lands and men, according to the fashion of the times, when men, being merely the live-stock of the land, were thrown into the bargain. If they were generous, it was not because they thought, with M. Thiers, that the Pope could not be independent without being a King; they had seen him in his poverty more independent and more commanding than almost any monarch on the earth. They enriched him from motives of friendship, calculation, gratitude, or it might even be to disinherit their relations, as we sometimes see in our own time. Since the days of the Countess Matilda, the Pope, having acquired a taste for possession, has gone on rounding his estate. He has obtained cities by capitulation, as in the case of Bologna; he has won others at the cannon's mouth, as Rimini; while some he has appropriated, by treachery and stealth, as Ancona. Indeed so well have matters been managed, that in 1859 the Bishop of Rome is the temporal sovereign of about six millions of acres, and reigns over three millions one hundred and twenty-four thousand six hundred and sixty-eight men, who are all crying out loudly against him.

What do they complain of? Only listen, and you will soon learn.

They say—that the authority to which, without having either asked or accepted it, they are subject, is the most fundamentally absolute that was ever defined by Aristotle; that the legislative, executive, and judicial powers are united, confounded, and jumbled together in one and the same hand, contrary to the practice of civilized states, and to the theory of Montesquieu; that they willingly recognize the infallibility of the Pope upon all religious questions, but that in civil matters it appears to them less easy to tolerate; that they do not refuse to obey, because, all things considered, man is not placed here below to follow the bent of his own inclinations, but that they would be glad to obey laws; that the good pleasure of any man, however good it may be, is not so good as the *Code Napoléon;* that the reigning Pope is not an evil-disposed man, but that the arbitrary government of one man, even admitting his infallibility, can never be anything but a bad government.

That in virtue of an ancient and hitherto ineradicable practice, the Pope is assisted in the temporal government of his States by the spiritual chiefs, subalterns, and spiritual *employés* of his Church; that Cardinals, Bishops, Canons,

Priests, forage pell-mell about the country; that one sole and identical caste possesses the right of administering both sacraments and provinces; of confirming little boys and the judgments of the lower courts; of ordaining subdeacons and arrests; of despatching parting souls and captains' commissions; that this confusion of the spiritual and the temporal disseminates among the higher offices a multitude of men, excellent no doubt in the sight of God, but insupportable in that of the people; often strangers to the country, sometimes to business, and always to those domestic ties which are the basis of every society; without any special knowledge, unless it be of the things of another world; without children, which renders them indifferent to the future of the nation; without wives, which renders them dangerous to its present; and to conclude, unwilling to hear reason, because they believe themselves participators in the pontifical infallibility.

That these servants of a most merciful but sometimes severe God, simultaneously abuse both mercy and justice; that, full of indulgence for the indifferent, for their friends, and for themselves, they treat with extreme rigour whoever has had the misfortune to become obnoxious to power; that they more readily pardon the wretch who cuts a man's throat, than the imprudent citizen who blames an abuse.

That the Pope, and the Priests who assist him, not having been taught accounts, grossly mismanage the public finances; that whereas maladministration or malversation of the public finances might have been tolerated a hundred years ago, when the expenses of public worship and of the papal court were defrayed by one hundred and thirty-nine millions of Catholics, it is a widely different affair now, when they have to be supported by 3,124,668 individuals.

That they do not complain of paying taxes, because it is a universally established practice, but that they wish to see their money spent upon terrestrial objects; that the sight of basilicas, churches, and convents built or maintained at their expense, rejoices them as Catholics, but grieves them as citizens, because, after all, these edifices are but imperfect substitutes for railways and roads, for the clearing of rivers, and the erection of dykes against inundations; that faith, hope, and charity receive more encouragement than agriculture, commerce, and manufactures; that public simplicity is developed to the detriment of public education.

That the law and the police are too much occupied with the salvation of souls, and too little with the preservation of bodies; that they prevent honest people from damning themselves by swearing, reading bad books, or associating with Liberals, but that they don't prevent rascals from murdering honest people; that property is as badly protected as persons; and that it is very hard to be able to reckon upon nothing for certain but a stall in Paradise.

That they are made to pay heavily for keeping up an army without knowledge or discipline, an army of problematical courage and doubtful honours, and destined never to fight except against the citizens themselves; that it is adding insult to injury to make a man pay for the stick he is beaten with. That they are moreover obliged to lodge foreign armies, and especially Austrians, who, as Germans, are notoriously heavy-fisted.

To conclude, they say all this is not what the Pope promised them in his *motu proprio* of the 19th of September; and it is sad to find infallible people breaking their most sacred engagements.

I have no doubt these grievances are exaggerated. It is impossible to believe that an entire nation can be so terribly in the right against its masters. We will examine the facts of the case in detail before we decide. We have not yet arrived at that point.

You have just heard the language, if not of the whole 3,124,668 people, at least of the most intelligent, the most energetic, and the most interesting part of the nation. Take away the conservative party,—that is to say, those who have an interest in the government,—and the unfortunate creatures whom it has utterly brutalized,—and there will remain none but malcontents.

The malcontents are not all of the same complexion. Some politely and vainly ask the Holy Father to reform abuses: this is the moderate party. Others propose to themselves a thorough reform of the government: they are called radicals, revolutionists, or Mazzinists—rather an injurious term. This latter category is not precisely nice as to the measures to be resorted to. It holds, with the Society of Jesus, that the end justifies the means. It says, if Europe leaves it *tête-à-tête* with the Pope, it will begin by cutting his throat; and if foreign potentates oppose such criminal violence, it will fling bombs under their carriages.

The moderate party expresses itself plainly, the Mazzinists noisily. Europe must be very stupid, not to understand the one; very deaf, not to hear the other.

What then happens?

All the States which desire peace, public order, and civilization, entreat the Pope to correct some abuse or other. "Have pity," they say, "if not upon your subjects, at least upon your neighbours, and save *us* from the conflagration!"

As often as this intervention is renewed, the Pope sends for his Secretary of State. The said Secretary of State is a Cardinal who reigns over the Holy Father in temporal matters, even as the Holy Father reigns over a hundred and thirty-nine millions of Catholics in spiritual matters. The Pope confides to the Cardinal Minister the source of his embarrassment, and asks him what is to be done.

The Cardinal, who is the minister of everything in the State, replies, without a moment's hesitation, to the old sovereign :—" In the first place, there are no abuses: in the next place, if there were any, we must not touch them. To reform anything is to make a concession to the malcontents. To give way, is to prove that we are afraid. To admit fear, is to double the strength of the enemy, to open the gates to revolution, and to take the road to Gaeta, where the accommodation is none of the best. Don't let us leave home. I know the house we live in; it is not new, but it will last longer than your Holiness—provided no attempt is made to repair it. After us the deluge; we've got no children!"

"All very true," replies the Pope. "But the sovereign who is entreating me to do something, is an eldest son of the Church. He has rendered us great services. He still protects us constantly. What would become of us if he abandoned us?"

"Don't be alarmed," says the Cardinal. "I'll arrange the matter diplomatically." And he sits down, and writes an invariable note, in a diplomatically tortuous style, which may thus be summed up :—

"We want your soldiers, and not your advice, seeing that we are infallible. If you were to show any symptom of doubting that infallibility, and if you attempted to force anything upon us, even our preservation, we would fold our wings around our countenances, we would raise the palms of martyrdom, and we should become an object of compassion to all the Catholics in the universe. You know we have in your country forty thousand men who are at liberty to say everything, and whom you pay with your own money to plead our cause. They shall preach to your subjects, that you are tyrannizing over the Holy Father, and we shall set your country in a blaze without appearing to touch it."

CHAPTER II.

NECESSITY OF THE TEMPORAL POWER.

"For the Pontificate there is no independence but sovereignty itself. Here is an interest of the highest order, which ought to silence the particular interests of nations, even as in a State the public interest silences individual interests."

These are not my words, but the words of M. Thiers: they occur in his report to the Legislative Assembly, in October 1849. I have no doubt this Father of the temporal Church expressed the wishes of one hundred and thirty-nine millions of Catholics. It was all Catholicity which said to 3,124,668 Italians, by the lips of the honourable reporter: "Devote yourselves as one man. Our chief can only be venerable, august, and independent, so long as he reigns despotically over you. If, in an evil hour, he were to cease wearing a crown of gold; if you were to contest his right to make and break laws; if you were to give up the wholesome practice of laying at his feet that money which he disburses for our edification and our glory, all the sovereigns of the universe would look upon him as an inferior. Silence, then, the noisy chattering of your individual interests."

I flatter myself that I am as fervent a Catholic as M. Thiers himself; and were I bold enough to seek to refute him, I should do it in the name of our common faith.

I grant you—this would be the tenor of my argument—

that the Pope ought to be independent. But could he not be so at a somewhat less cost? Is it absolutely necessary that 3,124,668 men should sacrifice their liberty, their security, and all that is most precious to them, in order to secure the independence which makes us so happy and so proud? The Apostles were certainly independent at a cheaper rate, for they did nobody harm. The most independent of men is he who has nothing to lose. He pursues his own path, without troubling himself about powers and principalities, for the simple reason that the conqueror most bent on acquisition can take nothing from him.

The greatest conquests of Catholicism were made at a time when the Pope was not a ruler. Since he has become a king, you may measure the territory won from the Church by inches.

The earliest Popes, who were not kings, had no budgets. Consequently they had no annual deficits to make up. Consequently they were not obliged to borrow millions of M. de Rothschild. Consequently they were more independent than the crowned Popes of more recent times.

Ever since the spiritual and the temporal have been joined, like two Siamese powers, the most august of the two has necessarily lost its independence. Every day, or nearly so, the Sovereign Pontiff finds himself called upon to choose between the general interests of the Church, and the private interests of his crown. Think you he is sufficiently estranged from the things of this world to sacrifice heroically the earth, which is near, to the Heaven, which is remote? Besides, we have history to help us I might, if I chose, refer to certain bad Popes who were capable of selling the dogma of the Holy Trinity for half-a-dozen leagues of territory; but it would be hardly fair to argue from bad Popes to the confusion of indifferent ones. Think you, however, that when the

Pope legalized the perjury of Francis the First after the treaty of Madrid, he did it to make the morality of the Holy See respected, or to stir up a war useful to his crown?

When he organized the traffic in indulgences, and threw one-half of Europe into heresy, was it to increase the number of Christians, or to give a dowry to a young lady?

When, during the Thirty Years' War, he made an alliance with the Protestants of Sweden, was it to prove the disinterestedness of the Church, or to humble the House of Austria?

When he excommunicated Venice in 1806, was it to attach the Republic more firmly to the Church, or to serve the rancour of Spain against the first allies of Henry IV.?

When he suppressed the Order of the Jesuits, was it to reinforce the army of the Church, or to please his master in France?

When he terminated his relations with the Spanish American provinces upon their proclaiming their independence, was it in the interest of the Church, or of Spain?

When he held excommunication suspended over the heads of such Romans as took their money to foreign lotteries, was it to attach their hearts to the Church, or to draw their crown-pieces into his own treasury?

M. Thiers knows all this better than I do; but he possibly thought that when the spiritual sovereign of the Church and the temporal sovereign of a little country, wear the same cap, the one is naturally condemned to minister to the ambition or the necessities of the other.

We wish the chief of the Catholic religion to be independent, and we make him pay slavish obedience to a petty Italian prince; thus rendering the future of that religion subordinate to miserable local interests and petty parish squabbles.

But this union of powers, which would gain by separation, compromises not only the independence, but the dignity of the Pope. The melancholy obligation to govern men obliges him to touch many things which he had better leave alone. Is it not deplorable that bailiffs must seize a debtor's property in the Pope's name?—that judges must condemn a murderer to death in the name of the Head of the Church?—that the executioner must cut off heads in the name of the Vicar of Christ? There is to me something truly scandalous in the association of those two words, *Pontifical lottery!* And what can the hundred and thirty-nine millions of Catholics think, when they hear their spiritual sovereign expressing, through his finance minister, his satisfaction at the progress of vice as proved by the success of the lotteries?

The subjects of the Pope are not scandalized at these contradictions, simply because they are accustomed to them. They strike a foreigner, a Catholic, a casual unit out of the hundred and thirty-nine millions; they inspire in him an irresistible desire to defend the independence and the dignity of the Church. But the inhabitants of Bologna or Viterbo, of Terracina or Ancona, are more occupied with national than with religious interests, either because they want that feeling of self-devotion recommended by M. Thiers, or because the government of the priests has given them a horror of Heaven. Very middling Catholics, but excellent citizens, they everywhere demand the freedom of their country. The Bolognese affirm that they are not necessary to the independence of the Pope, which they say could do as well without Bologna as it has for some time contrived to do without Avignon. Every city repeats the same thing, and if they were all to be listened to, the Holy Father, freed from the cares of administration, might devote his undivided attention to the interests of the Church and the embellishment of Rome. The Romans themselves, so they be neither princes, nor priests, nor servants, nor beggars, declare that they have devoted themselves long enough, and that M. Thiers may now carry his advice elsewhere.

CHAPTER III.

THE PATRIMONY OF THE TEMPORAL POWER.

THE Papal States have no natural limits: they are carved out on the map as the chance of passing events has made them, and as the good-nature of Europe has left them. An imaginary line separates them from Tuscany and Modena. The most southerly point enters into the kingdom of Naples; the province of Benevento is enclosed within the states of King Ferdinand, as formerly was the Comtat-Venaissin within the French territory. The Pope, in his turn, shuts in that Ghetto of democracy, the republic of San Marino.

I never cast my eyes over this poor map of Italy, capriciously rent into unequal fragments, without one consoling reflection.

Nature, which has done everything for the Italians, has taken care to surround their country with magnificent barriers. The Alps and the sea protect it on all sides, isolate it, bind it together as a distinct body, and seem to design it for an individual existence. To crown all, no internal barrier condemns the Italians to form separate nations. The Apennines are so easily crossed, that the people on either side can speedily join hands. All the existing boundaries are entirely arbitrary, traced by the brutality of the Middle Ages, or the shaky hand of diplomacy, which undoes to-morrow what it does to-day. A single race covers the soil; the same language is spoken from north to south; the people are all united in a common bond by the glory of their ancestors, and the recollections of Roman conquest, fresher and more vivid than the hatreds of the fourteenth century.

These considerations induce me to believe that the people of Italy will one day be independent of all others, and united among themselves by the force of geography and history, two powers more invincible than Austria.

But I return *à mes moutons*, and to their shepherd, the Pope.

The kingdom possessed by a few priests, covers an extent, in round numbers, of six millions of acres, according to the statistics published in 1857 by Monsignor, now Cardinal, Milesi.

No country in Europe is more richly gifted, or possesses greater advantages, whether for agriculture, manufacture, or commerce.

Traversed by the Apennines, which divide it about equally, the Papal dominions incline gently, on one side to the Adriatic, on the other to the Mediterranean. In each of these seas they possess an excellent port: to the east, Ancona; to the west, Civita Vecchia. If Panurge had had Ancona and Civita Vecchia in his Salmagundian kingdom, he would infallibly have built himself a navy. The Phœnicians and the Carthaginians were not so well off.

A river, tolerably well known under the name of the Tiber, waters nearly the whole country to the west. In former days it ministered to the wants of internal commerce. Roman historians describe it as navigable up to Perugia. At the present time it is hardly so as far as Rome; but if its bed were cleared out, and filth not allowed to be thrown in, it would render greater service, and would not overflow so often. The country on the other side is watered by small rivers, which, with a little government assistance, might be rendered very serviceable.

In the level country the land is of prodigious fertility. More than a fourth of it will grow corn. Wheat yields a return of fifteen for one on the best land, thirteen on middling, and nine on the worst. Fields thrown out of cultivation become admirable natural pastures. The hemp is of very fine quality when cultivated with care. The vine and the mulberry thrive wherever they are planted. The finest olive-trees and the best olives in Europe grow in the mountains. A variable, but generally mild climate, brings to maturity the products of extreme latitudes. Half the country is favourable to the palm and the orange. Numerous and thriving flocks roam across the plains in winter, and ascend to the mountains in summer. Horses, cows, and sheep live and multiply in the open air, without need of shelter. Indian buffaloes swarm in the marshes. Every species of produce requisite for the food and clothing of man grows easily, and as it were joyfully, in this privileged land. If men in the midst of it are in want of bread or shirts, Nature has no cause to reproach herself, and Providence washes its hands of the evil.

In all the three states raw material exists in incredible abundance. Here are hemp, for ropemakers, spinners, and weavers; wine, for distillers; olives, for oil and soap makers; wool, for cloth and carpet manufacturers; hides and skins, for tanners, shoemakers, and glovers; and silk in any quantity for manufactures of luxury. The iron ore is of middling quality, but the island of Elba, in which the very best is found, is near at hand. The copper and lead mines, which the ancients worked profitably, are perhaps not exhausted. Fuel is supplied by a million or two of acres of forest land; besides which, there is the sea, always open for the transport of coal from Newcastle. The volcanic soil of several provinces produces enormous quantities of sulphur, and the alum of Tolfi is the best in the world. The quartz of Civita Vecchia will give us kaolin for porcelain. The quarries contain building materials, such as marble and pozzolana, which is Roman cement almost ready-made.

In 1847, the country lands subject to the Pope were valued at about £34,800,000 sterling. The province of Benevento was not included, and the Minister of Commerce and Public Works admitted that the property was not estimated at above a third of its real value. If capital returned its proper interest, if activity and industry caused trade and manufactures to increase the national income as ought to be the case, it would be the Rothschilds who would borrow money of the Pope at six per cent. interest.

But stay! I have not yet completed the catalogue of possessions. To the present munificence of nature must be added the inheritance of the past. The poor Pagans of great Rome left all their property to the Pope who damns them.

They left him gigantic aqueducts, prodigious sewers, and roads which we find still in use, after twenty centuries of traffic. They left him the Coliseum, for his Capuchins to preach in. They left him an example of an administration without an equal in history. But the heritage was accepted without the responsibilities attached to it.

I will no longer conceal from you that this magnificent territory appeared to me in the first place most unworthily cultivated. From Civita Vecchia to Rome, a distance of some sixteen leagues, cultivation struck me in the light of a very rare accident, to which the soil was but little accustomed. Some pasture fields, some land in fallow, plenty of brambles, and, at long intervals, a field with oxen at plough: this is what the traveller will see in April. He will not even meet with the occasional forest which he finds in the most desert regions of Turkey. It seems as if man had swept across the land to destroy everything, and the soil had been then taken possession of by flocks and herds.

The country round Rome resembles the road from Civita Vecchia. The capital is girt by a belt of uncultivated, but not unfertile land. I used to walk in every direction, and sometimes for a long distance; the belt seemed very wide. However, in proportion as I receded from the city, I found the fields better cultivated. One would suppose that at a certain distance from St. Peter's the peasants worked with greater relish. The roads, which near Rome are detestable, became gradually better; they were more frequented, and the people I met seemed more cheerful. The inns became habitable, by comparison, in an astonishing degree. Still, so long as I remained in that part of the country towards the Mediterranean, of which Rome is the centre, and which is more directly subject to its influence, I found that the appearance of the land always left something to be desired. I sometimes fancied that these honest labourers worked as if they were afraid to make a noise, lest, by smiting the soil too deeply and too boldly, they should wake up the dead of past ages.

But when once I had crossed the Apennines, when I was beyond the reach of the breeze which blew over the capital, I began to inhale an atmosphere of labour and goodwill that cheered my heart. The fields were not only dug, but manured, and, still better, planted and sown. The smell of manure was quite new to me. I had never met with it on the other side of the Apennines. I was delighted at the sight of trees. There were rows of vines twining around elms planted in fields of hemp, wheat, or clover. In some places the vines and elms were replaced by mulberry-trees. What mingled riches were here lavished by nature! How bounteous is the earth! Here were mingled together, in rich profusion, bread, wine, shirts, silk gowns, and forage for the cattle. St. Peter's is a noble church, but, in its way, a well-cultivated field is a beautiful sight!

I travelled slowly to Bologna; the sight of the country I passed through, and the fruitfulness of honest human labour, made me happy. I retraced my steps towards St. Peter's; my melancholy returned when I found myself again amidst the desolation of the Roman Campagna.

As I reflected on what I had seen, a disquieting idea forced itself upon me in a geometrical form. It seemed to me that the activity and prosperity of the subjects of the Pope were in exact proportion to the square of the distance which separated them from Rome: in other words, that the shade of the monuments of the eternal city was noxious to the cultivation of the country. Rabelais says the shade of monasteries is fruitful; but he speaks in another sense.

I submitted my doubts to a venerable ecclesiastic, who hastened to undeceive me. "The country is not uncultivated," he said; "or if it be so, the fault is with the subjects of the Pope. This people is indolent by nature, although 21,415 monks are always preaching activity and industry to them!"

CHAPTER IV.

THE SUBJECTS OF THE TEMPORAL POWER.

On the 14th of May, 1856, M. de Rayneval, then French ambassador at Rome, a warm friend to the cardinals, and consequently a bitter foe to their subjects, thus described the Italian people :—

" A nation profoundly divided among themselves, animated by ardent ambition, possessing none of the qualities which constitute the greatness and power of others, devoid of energy, equally wanting in military spirit and in the spirit of association, and respecting neither the law nor social distinctions."

M. de Rayneval will be canonized a hundred years hence (if the present system continue) for having so nobly defended the oppressed.

It will not be foreign to my purpose to try my own hand at this picture; for the subjects of the Pope are Italians like the rest, and there is but one nation in the Italian peninsula. The difference of climate, the vicinity of foreigners, the traces of invasions, may have modified the type, altered the accent, and slightly varied the language; still the Italians are the same everywhere, and the middle class—the *élite* of every people—think and speak alike from Turin to Naples. Handsome, robust, and healthy, when the neglect of Governments has not delivered them over to the fatal *malaria*, the Italians are, mentally, the most richly endowed people in Europe. M. de Rayneval, who is not the man to flatter them, admits that they have "intelligence, penetration, and aptitude for everything." The cultivation of the arts is no less natural to them than is the study of the sciences; their first steps in every path open to human intellect are singularly rapid, and if but too many of them stop before the end is attained, it is because their success is generally barred by deplorable circumstances. In private as well as public affairs, they possess a quick apprehension and sagacity carried to suspicion. There is no race more ready at making and discussing laws; legislation and jurisprudence have been among their chief triumphs. The idea of law sprang up in Italy at the time of the foundation of Rome, and it is the richest production of this marvellous soil. The Italians still possess administrative genius in a high degree. Administration went forth from the midst of them for the conquest of the world, and the greatest administrators known to history, Cæsar and Napoleon, were of Italian origin.

Thus gifted by nature, they have the sense of their high qualities, and they at times carry it to the extent of pride. The legitimate desire to exercise the faculties they possess, degenerates into ambition; but their pride would not be ludicrous, nor would their ambition appear extravagant, if their hands were free for action. Through a long series of ages, despotic Governments have penned them into a narrow area. The impossibility of realizing high aims, and the want of action which perpetually stirs within them, has driven them to paltry disputes and local quarrels. Are we to infer from this that they are incapable of becoming a nation? I am not of that opinion. Already they are uniting to call upon the King of Piedmont, and to applaud the policy of Count Cavour. If this be not sufficient proof, make an experiment. Take away the barriers which separate them; I will answer for their soon being united. But the keepers of these barriers are the King of Naples, the Grand Duke of Tuscany, Austria, the Pope, and the rest. Are such keepers likely to give up the keys?

I know not what are "the qualities which constitute the greatness and power of other nations"—as, for example, the Austrian nation,—but I know very few qualities, physical, intellectual, or moral, which the Italians do not possess.

Are they "devoid of energy," as M. de Rayneval declares? I should rather repoach them with the opposite excess. The absurd but resolute defence of Rome against the French army, may surely be regarded as the act of an energetic people. We must be extremely humble, if we admit that a French army was held in check for two months by men wanting in energy. The assassinations which occur in the streets of Rome, prove rather the inefficiency of the police than the effeminacy of the citizens. I find, from an official return, that in 1853 the Roman tribunals punished 609 crimes against property, and 1,344 against the person. These figures do not indicate a faultless people, but they prove little inclination for base theft, and look rather like a diabolical energy. In the same year the Assize Courts in France pronounced judgment upon 3,719 individuals charged with theft, and 1,921 with crimes against the person. The proportion is reversed. Robbers have the majority with us. And yet we are rather an energetic people.

If the Italians are so also, there will not be much difficulty in making soldiers of them. M. de Rayneval tells us, they are "entirely wanting in military spirit." No doubt he echoed the opinion of some Cardinal. Indeed! Were the Piedmontese in the Crimea, then, wanting in the military spirit?

M. de Rayneval and the Cardinals are willing to admit the courage of the Piedmontese, but then, they say, Piedmont is not in Italy; its inhabitants are half Swiss, half French. Their language is not Italian, neither are their habits, the proof of which is found in the fact, that they have the true military and monarchical spirit, unknown to the rest of Italy. According to this, it would be far easier to prove that the Alsacians and the Bretons are not French; the first, because they are the best soldiers in the empire, and because they say *Meinherr* when we should say *Monsieur;* the second, because they have the true monarchical spirit, and because they call *butun* what we call *tabac.* But all the soldiers of Italy are not in Piedmont. The King of Naples has a good army. The Grand Duke of Tuscany has a sufficient one for his defence; the small Duchies of Modena and Parma have a smart regiment or two. Lombardy, Venice, Modena, and one-half of the Papal States, have given heroes to France. Napoleon remembered it at St. Helena; it has been so written.

As for the spirit of association, I know not where it is to be found, if not in Italy. By what is the Catholic world governed? By an Association. What is it but an Association that wastes the revenue of the poor Romans? Who monopolizes their corn, their hemp, their oil? Who lays waste the forests of the State? An Association. Who take possession of the highways, stop diligences, and lay travellers under contribution? Five or six Associations. Who keeps up agitation at Genoa, at Leghorn, and, above all, at Rome? That secret Association known as the Mazzinists.

I grant that the Romans have but a moderate respect for the law. But the truth is, there is no law in the country. They have a respect for the Code Napoléon, since they urgently ask for it. What they do not respect is, the official caprice of their masters. I am certainly no advocate of disorder; but when I think that a mere fancy of Cardinal Antonelli, scribbled on a sheet of paper, has the force of law for the present and the future, I can understand an insolent contempt of the laws, to the extent of actual revolt.

As for social distinctions, it strikes me that the Italians respect them even too much. When I have led you for half an hour through the streets of Rome, you will ask yourselves to what a Roman prince can possibly be superior. Nevertheless the Romans exhibit a sincere respect for their princes: habit is so strong! If I were to conduct you to the source of some of the large fortunes among my acquaintances, you would rise with stones and sticks against the superiority of wealth. And yet the Romans, dazzled by dollars, are full of respect for the rich. If I were to— But I think the Italian nation is sufficiently justified. I will but add, that if it is easily led to evil, it is still more easily brought back to good; that it is passionate and violent, but not ill-disposed, and that a kind act suffices to make it forget the most justifiable enmities.

I will add in conclusion, that the Italians are not enervated by the climate to such a degree as to dislike work. A traveller who may happen to have seen some street porters asleep in the middle of the day, returns home and informs Europe that these lazy people snore from morning till night; that they have few wants, and work just enough to keep themselves from one day to another. I shall presently show you that the labourers of the rural districts are as industrious as our own peasants (and that, too, in a very different temperature), as economical, provident, and orderly, though more hospitable and more charitable. If the lower orders in the towns have become addicted to extravagance, idleness, and mendicity, it is because they have discovered the impossibility, even by the most heroic efforts and the most rigid economy, of gaining either capital or independence or position. Let us not confound discouragement with want of courage, nor tax a poor fellow with idleness, merely because he has had the misfortune to be knocked down and run over by a carriage.

The Pope reigns over 3,124,668 souls, as I have already observed more than once. This population is unequally distributed over the surface of the country. The population in the provinces of the Adriatic is nearly double that in the Mediterranean provinces, and more immediately under the Sovereign's eyes.

Those pious economists who insist upon it that all is for the best under the most sacred of governments, will not scruple to tell you :—

"Our State is one of the most populous in Europe: *therefore* it must be one of the best governed. The average population of France is $67\frac{1}{2}$ inhabitants to the square kilomètre; that of the States of the Church $75\frac{7}{10}$. It follows from this that if the Emperor of the French were to adopt our mode of administration, he would have $8\frac{2}{10}$ inhabitants more on each square kilomètre!

"The province of Ancona, which is occupied by the Austrians, and governed by priests, has 155 inhabitants to the square kilomètre. The Bas-Rhin, which is the fourth department of France, has but 129, consequently it is evident that the Bas-Rhin will continue to be relatively inferior, so long as it is not governed by priests, and occupied by the Austrians.

"The population of our happy country became increased by one-third between the vears 1816 and 1853, a space of thirty-seven years. Such a grand result can only be attributed to the excellent administration of the Holy Father, and the preaching of 38,320 priests and monks, who protect youth from the destructive influence of the passions.*

"You will observe that the English have a passion for moving about the country. Even in the interior they change their residence and their county with an incredible mobility; no doubt this is because their country is unhealthy and badly administered. In the El Dorado which we govern, no more than 178,943 individuals are known to have changed their abode from one province to another: *therefore* our subjects are all happy in their homes."

I do not deny the eloquence of these figures, and I am not one of those who think statistics prove everybody's case. But it seems to me very natural that a rich country, in the hands of an agricultural people, should feed 75 inhabitants to the square kilomètre, under any sort of government. What astonishes me is that it should feed no more; and I promise you that when it is better governed it will feed many more.

The population of the States of the Church has increased by one-third in thirty-seven years. But that of Greece has trebled between 1832 and 1853. Nevertheless Greece is in the enjoyment of a detestable government; as I believe I have pretty correctly demonstrated elsewhere.† The increase of a population proves the vitality of a race rather than the solicitude of an administration. I will never believe that 770,000 children were born between 1816 and 1853 by the intervention of the priests. I prefer to believe that the Italian race is vigorous, moral, and marriageable, and that it does not yet despair of the future.

* Preface to the Official Statistical Returns of 1853, page 64.

† 'La Grèce Contemporaine.'

Lastly, if the subjects of the Pope stay at home, instead of moving about, it may be because communication between one place and another is difficult, or because the authorities are close-fisted in the matter of passports; it may be, too, because they are certain of finding, in whatever part of the country they move to, the same priests, the same judges, and the same taxes.

Out of the population of 3,124,668 souls, more than a million are agricultural labourers and shepherds. The workmen number 258,872, and the servants exceed the workmen by about 30,000. Trade, finance, and general business occupy something under 85,000 persons.

The landed proprietors are 206,558 in number, being about one-fifteenth of the entire population. We have a greater proportion in France. The official statistics of the Roman State inform us that if the national wealth were equally divided among all the proprietors, each of the 206,558 families would possess a capital of £680 sterling. But they have omitted to state that some of these landed proprietors possess 50,000 acres, and others a mere heap of flints.

It is to be observed that the division of land, like all other good things, increases in proportion to the distance from the capital. In the province of Rome there are 1,956 landed proprietors out of 176,002 inhabitants, which is about one in ninety. In the province of Macerata, towards the Adriatic, there are 39,611, out of 243,104, or one proprietor to every six inhabitants, which is as much as to say that in this province there are almost as many properties as there are families.

The Agro Romano, which it took Rome several centuries to conquer, is at the present time the property of 113 families, and of 64 corporations.*

* Etudes Statistiques sur Rome, par le Comte de Tournon.

CHAPTER V.

OF THE PLEBEIANS.

The subjects of the Holy Father are divided by birth and fortune into three very distinct classes,—nobility, citizens, and people, or plebeians. The Gospel has omitted to consecrate the inequality of men, but the law of the State—that is to say, the will of the Popes—carefully maintains it. Benedict XIV. declared it honourable and salutary in his Bull of January 4, 1746, and Pius IX. expressed himself in the same terms at the beginning of his *Chirografo* of May 2, 1853.

If I do not reckon the clergy among the classes of society, it is because that body is foreign to the nation by its interests, by its privileges, and often by its origin. The Cardinals and Prelates are not, properly speaking, the Pope's subjects, but rather his ghostly confederates, and the partners of his omnipotence.

The distinction of class is more especially perceptible at Rome, near the Pontifical throne. It gradually disappears, together with many other abuses, in proportion to their distance from their source. There are bottomless abysses between the noble Roman and the citizen of Rome, between the citizen of Rome and the plebeian of the city. The plebeian himself discharges a portion of the scorn expressed by the two superior classes for himself, upon the peasants he meets at market: it is a sort of cascade of contempt. At Rome, thanks to the traditions of history, and the education given by the Popes, the inferior thinks he can get out of his nothingness, and become something, by begging the favour and support of a superior. A general system of dependence and patronage makes the plebeian kneel before the man of the middle class, who again kneels before the prince, who in his turn kneels more humbly than all the others before the sovereign clergy.

At twenty leagues' distance from Rome there is very little kneeling; beyond the Apennines none at all. When you reach Bologna you find an almost French equality in the manners: for the simple reason that Napoleon has left his mark there.

The absolute value of the men in each category increases according to the square of the distance. You may feel almost certain that a Roman noble will be less educated, less capable, and less free than a gentleman of the Marches or of the Romagna. The middle class, with some exceptions which I shall presently mention, is infinitely more numerous, more enlightened, and wealthier, to the east of the Apennines, than in and about the capital. The plebeians themselves have more honesty and morality when they live at a respectful distance from the Vatican.

The plebeians of the Eternal City are overgrown children badly brought up, and perverted in various ways by their education. The Government, which, being in the midst of them, fears them, treats them mildly. It demands few taxes of them; it gives them shows, and sometimes bread, the *panem et circenses* prescribed by the Emperors of the Decline. It does not teach them to read, neither does it forbid them to beg. It sends Capuchins to their homes. The Capuchin gives the wife lottery-tickets, drinks with the husband, and brings up the children after his kind, and sometimes in his likeness. The plebeians of Rome are certain never to die of hunger; if they have no bread, they are allowed to help themselves from the baker's basket; the law allows it. All that is required of them is to be good Christians, to prostrate themselves before the priests, to humble themselves before the rich, and to abstain from revolutions. They are severely punished if they refuse to take the Sacrament at Easter, or if they talk disrespectfully of the Saints. The tribunal of the Vicariates listens to no excuses on this head; but the police is enough as to everything else. Crimes are forgiven them, they are encouraged in meanness; the only offences for which there is no pardon are the cry for liberty, revolt against an abuse, the assertion of manhood.

It is marvellous to me that with such an education there is any good left in them at all. The worst half of the people is that which dwells in the Monti district. If, in seeking the Convent of the Neophytes, or the house of Lucrezia Borgia, you miss your way among those foul narrow streets, you will find yourself in the midst of a strange medley of thieves, sharpers, guitar-players, artists' models, beggars, *ciceroni*, and *ruffiani*. If you speak to them, you may be sure they will kiss your Excellency's hand, and pick your Excellency's pocket. I do not think a worse breed is to be found in any city in Europe, not even in London. All these people *practise* religion, without the least believing in God. The police does not meddle much with them. To be sure they are sent to prison now and then, but thanks to a favourable word in the right quarter, or to the want of prison accommodation, they are soon set at liberty. Even the honest workmen their neighbours occasionally get into scrapes. They have made plenty of money in the winter, and spent it all in the Carnival—as is the common custom. Summer comes, the foreign visitors depart; no more work and no more money. Moral training, which might sustain them, is wholly wanting. The love of show, that peculiar disease of Rome, is their bane. The wife, if she be pretty, sells herself, or the husband does what he had better leave undone.

Judge them not too harshly. Remember, they have read nothing, they have never been out of Rome; the example of ostentation is set them by the Cardinals, of misconduct by the prelates, of venality by the different functionaries, of squandering by the Finance Minister. And above all, remember that care has been taken to root out from their hearts, as if it were a destructive weed, that noble sentiment of human dignity which is the principle of every virtue.

The blood which flows in Italian veins must be very generous, or so notable a portion of the plebeians of Rome as the people of the *Trastevere*, could never have preserved their manly virtues, as is notoriously the case with them. I have met with men in this quarter of the city, coarse, violent, sometimes ferocious, but really *men;* nice as to their honour, to the extent of poniarding any one who is wanting in respect to them. They are fully as ignorant as the people of the Monti; they have learnt the same lessons, and witnessed the same examples; they have the same improvidence, the same love of pleasure, the same brutality in their passions; but they are incapable of stooping, even to pick anything up.

A government worthy of the name would make something of this ignorant force, first taming, and then directing it. The man who stabs his fellow in a wineshop might prove a good soldier on a battle-field. But we are in the capital of the Pope. The Trasteverini neither attack God nor the Government; they meddle neither with theology nor politics; no more is asked of them. And in token of its appreciation of their good conduct, a paternal administration allows them to cut one another's throats *ad libitum.*

Neither the people of the Trastevere nor of the Monti give the least sign of political existence, whereat the Cardinals rub their hands, and congratulate themselves upon having kept so many men in profound ignorance of all their rights. I am not quite certain that the theory is a sound one. Suppose, for example, that the democratic committees of London and Leghorn were to send a few recruiting officers into the Pope's capital. An honest, mild, enlightened plebeian would reflect twice before enrolling himself. He would weigh the pros and the cons, and balance for a long time between the vices of the government, and the dangers of revolution. But the mob of the Monti would take fire like a heap of straw at the mere prospect of a scramble, while the Trastevere savages would rise to a man, if the Papal despotism were represented to them as an attack upon their honour. It would be better to have in these plebeians foes capable of reasoning. The Pope might often have to reckon with them, but he need never tremble before them.

I trust the masters of the country may never more be obliged to fight with the plebeians of Rome. They were easily carried away by the leaders of 1848, although the name of Republic resounded for the first time in their ears. Have they forgotten it? No. They will long remember that magic word, which abased the great, and exalted the humble. Moreover, the hidden Mazzinists, who agitate throughout the city, don't collect the workmen in the quarter of the *Regola* to preach submission to them.

I have said that the plebeians of the city of Rome despise the plebeians of the country. Be assured, however, the latter are not deserving of scorn, even in the Mediterranean provinces. In this unhappy half of the Pontifical States, the influence of the Vatican has not yet quite morally destroyed the population. The country people are poor, ignorant, superstitious, rather wild, but kind, hospitable, and generally honest. If you wish to study them more closely, go to one of the villages in the province of Frosinone, towards the Neapolitan frontier. Cross the plains which malaria has made dreary solitudes, take the stony path which winds painfully up the side of the mountain. You will come to a town of five or ten thousand souls, which is little more than a dormitory for five or ten thousand peasants. Viewed from a distance, this country town has an almost grand appearance. The dome of a church, a range of monastic buildings, the tower of a feudal castle, invest it with a certain air of importance. A troop of women are coming down to the fountain with copper vessels on their heads. You smile instinctively. Here is movement and life. Enter! You are struck with a sensation of coldness, dampness, and darkness. The streets are narrow flights of steps, which every now and then plunge beneath low arches. The houses are closed, and seem to have been deserted for a century. Not a human being at the doors, or at the windows. The streets, silent and solitary.

You would imagine that the curse of heaven had fallen on the country, but for the large placards on the house-fronts, which prove that missionary fathers have passed through the place. "*Viva Gesù! Viva Maria! Viva il sangue di Gesù! Viva il cor di Maria! Bestemmiatori, tacetevi per l'amor di Maria!*"

These devotional sentences are like so many signboards of the public simplicity.

A quarter of an hour's walk brings you to the principal square. Half-a-dozen civil officials are seated in a circle before a café, gaping at one another. You join them. They ask you for news of something that happened a dozen years ago. You ask them in turn, what epidemic has depopulated the country?

Presently some thirty market-men and women begin to display on the pavement an assortment of fruit and vegetables. Where are the buyers of these products of the earth? Here they come! Night is approaching. The entire population begins to return at once from their labour in the fields; a stalwart and sturdy population; the thew and sinew of some fine regiments. Every one of these half-clad men, armed with pickaxe and shovel, rose two hours before the sun this morning, and went forth to weed a little field, or to dig round a few olive-trees. Many of them have their little domains several miles off, and thither they go daily, accompanied by a child and a pig. The pig is not very fat, and the man and his child are very lean. Still they seem light-hearted and merry. They have plucked some wild flowers by the roadside. The boy is crowned with roses, like Lucullus at table. The father buys a handful of vegetables, and a cake of maize, which will furnish the family supper. They will sleep well enough on this diet—if the fleas allow them. If you like to follow these poor people home, they will give you a kindly welcome, and will not fail to ask you to partake of their modest meal. Their furniture is very simple, their conversation limited; their heads are as well furnished as their dwellings.

The wife who has been awaiting the return of her lord, will open the door to you. Of all useful animals, the wife is the one which the Roman peasant employs most profitably. She makes the bread and the cakes; she spins, weaves, and sews; she goes every day three miles for wood, and one and a half for water; she carries a mule's load on her head; she works from sunrise to sunset, without question or complaint. Her numerous children are in themselves a precious resource: at four years old they are able to tend sheep and cattle.

It is vain to ask these country people what is their opinion of Rome and the government: their idea of these matters is infinitely vague and shadowy. The Government manifests itself to them in the person of an official, who, for the sum of three pounds sterling per month, administers and sells justice among them. This individual is the only gift Rome has ever conferred upon them. In return for the great benefit of his presence, they pay taxes on a tolerably extensive scale: so much for the house, so much for the live-stock, so much for the privilege of lighting a fire, so much on the wine, and so much on the meat—when they are able to enjoy that luxury. They grumble, though not very bitterly, regarding the taxes as a sort of periodical hailstorm falling on their year's harvest. If they were to learn that Rome had been swallowed up by an earthquake, they certainly would not put on mourning. They would go forth to their fields as usual, they would sell their crops for the usual price, and they would pay less taxes. This is what all towns inhabited by peasants think of the metropolis. Every township lives by itself, and for itself; it is an isolated body, which has arms to work, and a belly to fill. The cultivator of the land is everything, as was the case in the Middle Ages. There is neither trade, nor manufactures, nor business on any extended scale, nor movement of ideas, nor political life, nor any of those powerful bonds which, in well-governed countries, link the provincial towns to the capital, as the members to the heart.

If there be a capital for these poor people, it is Paradise. They believe in it fervently, and strive to attain it with all their might. The very peasant who grudges the State two crowns for his hearth-tax, willingly pays two and a half to have *Viva Maria* scrawled over his door. Another complains of the £3 per month paid to the Government official, without a murmur at the thirty priests supported by the township. There is a gentle disease which consoles them for all their ills, called Faith. It does not restrain them from dealing a stab with a knife, when the wine is in their brains, or rage in their hearts; but it will always prevent them from eating meat on a Friday.

If you would see them in all the ardour of their simplicity, you must visit the town on the day of a grand festival. Everybody, men, women, and children are rushing to the church. A carpet of flowers is spread along the road. Every countenance is glowing with excitement. What is the meaning of it all? Don't you know?—It is the festival of Sant' Antonio. A musical Mass is being performed in honour of Sant' Antonio. A grand procession is being formed in honour of that Saint, probably the patron of the place. There are little boys dressed up as angels, and men arrayed in the sack-like garment of their brotherhoods: here we have peasants of THE HEART OF JESUS; here, those of THE NAME OF MARY; and here come THE SOULS OF PURGATORY. The procession is formed with some little confusion. The people embrace one another, upset one another, and fight with one another—all in the name of Sant' Antonio. But see! The statue of the worthy Saint is coming out of the church: a wooden doll, with flaming red cheeks. *Victoria!* Off go the petards! The women weep with joy—the children cry out at the top of their shrill voices, "*Viva Sant' Antonio!*" At night there are fireworks: a balloon shaped in the semblance of the Saint ascends amid the shouts of the people, and bursts in grand style right over the church. Verily, unless Sant' Antonio be very difficult to please, such homage must go straight to his heart. And I should think the plebeians of the country very exacting, if, after such an intoxicating festival, they were to complain of wanting bread.

Let us seek a little repose on the other side of the Apennines. Although the population may not be sufficiently sheltered by a chain of mountains, you will find in the towns and villages the stuff for a noble nation. The ignorance is still very great; the blood ever boiling, and the hand ever quick; but already we find men who reason. If the workman of the towns be not successful, he guesses the reason; he seeks a remedy, he looks forward, he economizes. If the tenant be not rich, he studies with his landlord the means of becoming so. Everywhere agriculture is making progress, and it will ere long have no further progress to make. Man becomes better and greater by dint of struggling with Nature. He learns his own value, he sees whither he is tending; in cultivating his field, he cultivates himself.

I am compelled in strict truth to admit that religion loses ground a little in these fine provinces. I vainly sought in the towns of the Adriatic for those mural inscriptions of *Viva Gesù! Viva Maria!* and so on, which had so edified me on the other side of the Apennines. At Bologna I read sonnets at the corners of all the streets,—sonnet to Doctor Massarenti, who cured Madame Tagliani; sonnet to young Guadagni, on the occasion of his becoming Bachelor of Arts, etc., etc. At Faenza, these mural inscriptions evinced a certain degree of fanaticism, but the fanaticism of the dramatic art: *Viva la Ristori! Viva la diva Rossi!* At Rimini, and at Forlì, I read *Viva Verdi!* (which words had not then the political significance they have recently attained,) *Viva la Lotti!* together with a long list of dramatic and musical celebrities.

While I was visiting the holy house of Loretto, which, as

all the world knows, or ought to know, was transported by Angels, furniture and all, from Palestine, to the neighbourhood of Ancona, a number of pilgrims came in upon their knees, shedding tears and licking the flags with their tongues. I thought these poor creatures belonged to some neighbouring village, but I found out my mistake from a workman of Ancona, who happened to be near me. "Sir," he said, "these unhappy people must certainly belong to the other side of the Apennines, since they still make pilgrimages. Fifty years ago we used to do the same thing; we now think it better to work!"

CHAPTER VI.

THE MIDDLE CLASSES.

The middle class is, in every clime and every age, the foundation of the strength of States. It represents not only the wealth and independence, but the capacity and the morality of a people. Between the aristocracy, which boasts of doing nothing, and the lower orders who only work that they may not die of hunger, the middle class advances boldly to a future of wealth and consideration. Sometimes the upper class is hostile to progress, through fear of its results; too often the lower class is indifferent to it, from ignorance of the benefits it confers. The middle class has never ceased to tend towards progress, with all its strength, by an irresistible impulse, and even at the peril of its dearest interests. A great statesman who must be judged by his doctrines, and not by the chance of circumstances, M. Guizot, has shown us that the Roman Empire perished from the want of a middle class in the fifth century of our era, and we ourselves know with what impetuosity France has advanced in progress since the middle class revolution of 1789.

The middle class has not only the privilege of bringing about useful revolutions, it also claims the honour of repressing popular outbreaks, and opposing itself as a barrier to the overflow of evil passions.

It is to be desired, then, that this honourable class should become as numerous and as powerful as possible in the country we are now studying; because, while on the one hand it is the lawful heir of the temporal power of the Popes, on the other, it is the natural adversary of Mazzinist insurrection.

But the ecclesiastical caste, which sets this fatal principle of temporal power above the highest interests of society, can conceive nothing more prudent or efficacious than to vilify and abuse the middle class. It obliges this class to support the heaviest share of the budget, without being admitted to a share in the benefits. It takes from the small proprietor not only his whole income, but a part of his capital, while the people and the nobility are allowed all sorts of immunities. It demands heavy concessions in exchange for the humblest official posts. It omits no opportunity of depriving the liberal professions of all the importance they enjoy in other countries. It does its best to accelerate the decline of science and art. It imagines that nothing else can be abased, without its being proportionately elevated.

This system has succeeded (according to priestly notions) tolerably well at Rome and in the Mediterranean provinces, but very badly at Bologna, and in the Apennine provinces. In the metropolis of the country the middle class is reduced, impoverished, and submissive; in the second capital it is much more numerous, wealthy, and independent. But evil passions, far more fatal to society than the rational resistance of parties, have progressed in an inverse direction. They predominate but little at Bologna, where the middle class is strong enough to keep them under; they triumph at Rome, where the middle class has been destroyed. Thence it follows that Bologna is a city of opposition, and Rome a socialist city; and that the revolution will be moderate at Bologna, sanguinary at Rome. This is what the clerical party has gained.

Nothing can equal the disdain with which the prelates the princes, the foreigners of condition, and even the footmen at Rome, judge the middle class, or MEZZO CETO.

The prelate has his reasons. If he be a minister, he sees in his offices some hundred clerks, belonging to the middle class. He knows that these active and intelligent, but underpaid men, are for the most part obliged to eke out a livelihood by secretly following some other occupation: one keeps the books of a land-steward, another those of a Jew. Whose fault is it? They well know that neither excellence of character nor length of service are carried to the credit of the civil functionary, and that, after having earned advancement, he will be obliged either to ask it himself as a favour, or to employ the intercession of his wife. It is not these poor men whom we should despise, but the dignitaries in violet stockings who impose the burden upon them.

Should Monsignore be a judge of a superior tribunal, of the SACRA ROTA for instance, he need know nothing about the law. His secretary, or assistant, has by dint of patient study made himself an accomplished lawyer, as indeed a man must be who can thread his way through the dark labyrinths of Roman legislation. But Monsignore, who makes use of his assistant's ability for his own particular profit, thinks he has a right to despise him, because he is ill paid, lives humbly, and has no future to look forward to. Which of the two is in the wrong?

If the same prelate be a Judge of Appeal, he will profess a most profound contempt for advocates. I must confess they are to be pitied, these unfortunate Princes of the Bar, who write for the blind, and speak to the deaf, and who wear out their shoes in treading the interminable paths of Rotal procedure. But assuredly they are not men to be despised. They have always knowledge, often eloquence.

Marchetti, Rossi, and Lunati might no doubt have written good sermons, if they had not preferred doing something else.

Between ourselves, I think the prelates affect to despise them, in order that they may not have to fear them. They have condemned some of them to exile, others to silence and want. Hear what Cardinal Antonelli said to M. de Gramont :—

" The advocates used to be one of our sores ; we are beginning to be cured of it. If we could but get rid of the clerks in the offices, all would go well."

Let us hope that, among modern inventions, a bureaucratic machine may be made by which the labour of men in offices may be superseded.

The Roman princes affect to regard the middle class with contempt. The advocate who pleads their causes, and generally gains them, belongs to the middle class. The physician who attends them, and generally cures them, belongs to the middle class. But as these professional men have fixed salaries, and as salaries resemble wages, contempt is thrown into the bargain. Still the contempt is a magnanimous sort of contempt—that of a patron for his client. At Paris, when an advocate pleads a prince's cause, it is the prince who is the client : at Rome, it is the advocate.

But the individual who is visited by the most withering contempt of the Roman princes is the farmer, or *mercante di campagna ;* and I don't wonder at it.

The *mercante di campagna* is an obscure individual, usually very honest, very intelligent, very active, and very rich. He undertakes to farm several thousand acres of land, pasture or arable as may be, which the prince would never be able to farm himself, because he neither knows how, nor has the means to do so. Upon this princely territory the farmer lets loose, in the most disrespectful manner, droves of bullocks, and cows, and horses, and flocks of sheep. Should his lease permit him, he cultivates a square league or so, and sows it with wheat. When harvest-time arrives, down from the mountains troop a thousand or twelve hundred peasants, who overrun the prince's land in the farmer's service. The corn is reaped, threshed in the open field, put into sacks, and carted away. The prince sees it go by, as he stands on his princely balcony. He learns that a man of the *mezzo ceto*, a man who passes his life on horseback, has harvested on his land so many sacks of corn, which have produced him so much money. The *mercante di campagna* comes, and confirms the intelligence, and then pays the rent agreed upon to the uttermost baioccho. Sometimes he even pays down a year or two in advance. What prince could forgive such aggravated insolence? It is the more atrocious, since the farmer is polite, well-mannered, and much better educated than the prince; he can give his daughters much larger fortunes, and could buy the entire principality for his own son, if by chance the prince were obliged to sell it. The cultivation of estates by means of these people is, in the eyes of the Roman princes, an attack upon the rights of property. Their passion for incessant work is a disturbance of the delightful Roman tranquillity. The fortunes they acquire by personal exertion, energy, and activity, are a reproach by inference to that stagnant wealth which is the foundation of the State, and the admiration of the Government.

This is not all: the *mercante di campagna*, who is not nobly born, who is not a priest, who has a wife and children, thinks he has a right to share in the management of the affairs of his country, upon the ground that he manages his own well. He points out abuses; he demands reforms.

What audacity! The priests would cast him forth as they would a mere advocate, were it not that his occupation is the most necessary of all occupations, and that by turning out a man they might starve a district.

But the insolence of these agricultural contractors goes still further. They presume to be grand in their ideas. One of them, in 1848, under the reign of Mazzini, when the public works were suspended for want of money, finished the bridge of Lariccia, one of the finest constructions of our time, at his own expense. He certainly knew not whether the Pope would ever return to Rome to repay him. He acted like a real prince; but his audacity in assuming a part which was not intended for his caste, merited something more than contempt.

I, who have not the honour to be a prince, have no reason to despise the *mercanti di campagna*. Quite the contrary. I have solid ones for esteeming them highly. I have found them full of intelligence, kindness, and cordiality: middle-class men in the best sense of the term. My sole regret is that their numbers are so few, and that their scope of action is so limited.

If there were but two thousand of them, and the Government allowed them to follow their own course, the Roman Campagna would soon assume another aspect, and fever and ague take themselves off.

The foreigners who have inhabited Rome for any length of time, speak of the middle-class as contemptuously as the princes. I once made the same mistake as they do, so my testimony on the subject is the more worthy of acceptation.

Perhaps the foreigners in question have lived in furnished lodgings, and have found the landlady a little less than cruel. No doubt adventures of this kind are of daily occurrence elsewhere than in Rome; but is the middle-class to be held responsible for the light conduct of some few poor and uneducated women?

Or they may have had to do with the trade of Rome, and have found it extremely limited. This is because there is no capital, nor any extension of public credit. They are shocked to see the shopkeepers, during the Carnival, riding in carriages, and occupying the best boxes at the theatres; but this foolish love of show, so hurtful to the middle-class, is taught them by the universal example of those above them.

Perhaps they have sent to the chemist's for a doctor, and have fallen upon an ignorant professor of the healing art. This is unlucky, but it may happen anywhere. The medical body is not recruited exclusively among the eagles of science. For one Baroni, who is an honour at once to Rome, to Italy, and to Europe, you naturally expect to find many blockheads. If these are more plentiful at Rome than at Paris or Bologna, it is because the priests meddle with medical instruction, as with everything else. I never shall forget how I laughed when I entered the amphitheatre of Santo Spirito, to see a vine-leaf on 'the subject' on which the professor was going to lecture to the students.

In this land of chastity, where the modest vine is entwined with every branch of science, a doctor in surgery, attached to an hospital, once told me he had never seen the bosom of a woman. "We have," he said, "two degrees of Doctor to take; one theoretical, the other practical. Between the first and the second, we practise in the hospitals, as you see. But the prelates who control our studies, will not allow a doctor to be present at a confinement until he has passed his second, or practical examination. They are afraid of our being scandalized. We obtain our practical knowledge of midwifery by practising upon dolls. In six months I shall have taken all my degrees, and I may be called in to act as accoucheur to any number of women, without ever having witnessed a single accouchement!"

The Roman artists would endow the middle-class with both fame and money, if they were differently treated. The Italian race has not degenerated, whatever its enemies and its masters may say: it is as naturally capable of distinction in all the arts as ever it was. Put a paint-brush into the hands of a child, and he will acquire the practice of painting in no time. An apprenticeship of three or four years enables him to gain a livelihood. The misfortune is, that they seldom get beyond this. I think, nay, I am almost sure, they are not less richly gifted than the pupils of Raphael; and they reach the same point as the pupils of M. Galimard. Is it their fault? No. I accuse but the medium into which their birth has cast them. It may be, that if they were at Paris, they would produce masterpieces. Give them parts to play in the world, competition, exhibitions, the support of a government, the encouragement of a public, the counsels of an enlightened criticism. All these benefits which we enjoy abundantly, are wholly denied to them, and are only known to them by hearsay.

Their sole motive for work is hunger, their sole encouragement the flying visits of foreigners. Their work is always done in a hurry; they knock off a copy in a week, and when it is sold, they begin another.

If some one, more ambitious than his fellows, undertakes an original work, whose opinion can he obtain as to its merits or demerits? The men of the reigning class know nothing about it, and the princes very little. The owner of the finest gallery in Rome said last year, in the salon of an Ambassador, "I admire nothing but what you French call *chic.*" Prince Piombino gave the painter Gagliardi an order to paint him a ceiling, and proposed to pay him by the day. The Government has plenty to attend to without encouraging the arts: the four little newspapers which circulate at remote periods amuse themselves by puffing their particular friends in the silliest manner.

The foreigners who come and go are often men of taste, but they do not make a public. In Paris, Munich, Düsseldorf, and London, the public has an individuality; it is a man of a thousand heads. When it has marked a rising artist, it notes his progress, encourages him, blames him, urges him on, checks him. It takes such a one into its favour, is extremely wroth with such another. It is, of course, sometimes in the wrong; it is subject to ridiculous infatuations, and unjust revulsions of feeling; yet it lives, and it vivifies, and it is worth working for.

If I wonder at anything, it is that under the present system such artists are to be found at Rome as Tenerani and Podesti, in statuary and painting; Castellani, in gold-working; Calamatta and Mercuri, in engraving, with some others. It is a melancholy truth, however, that the majority of Roman artists are doomed, by the absence of encouragement, to a monotonous and humiliating round of taskwork and trade; occupied half their time in re-copying copies, and the remainder in recommending their goods to the foreign purchaser.

In truth, I had myself quitted Rome with no very favourable idea of the middle class. A few distinguished artists, a few advocates of talent and courage, some able medical men, some wealthy and skilful farmers, were insufficient, in my opinion, to constitute a middle class. I regarded them as so many exceptions to a rule. And as it is certain that there can be no nation without a middle class, I dreaded lest I should be forced to admit that there is no Italian nation.

The middle class appeared to me to thrive no better in

the Mediterranean provinces than at Rome. Half citizen, half clown, the people representing it are plunged in a crass ignorance. Having just sufficient means to live without working, they lounge away their time in homes comfortless and half-furnished, the very walls of which seem to reek with *ennui*. Rumours of what is passing in Europe, which might possibly rouse them from their torpor, are stopped at the frontier. New ideas, which might somewhat fertilize their minds, are intercepted by the Custom House. If they read anything, it is the Almanack, or by way of a higher order of literature, the *Giornale di Roma*, wherein the daily rides of the Pope are pompously chronicled. The existence of these people consists, in short, of a round of eating, drinking, sleeping, and reproducing their kind, until death arrive.

But beyond the Apennines matters are far otherwise. There, instead of the citizen descending to the level of the peasant, it is the peasant who rises to that of the citizen. Unremitting labour is continually improving both the soil and man. A smuggling of ideas which daily becomes more active, sets custom-houses and customs officers at defiance. Patriotism is stimulated and kept alive by the presence of the Austrians. Common sense is outraged by the weight of taxation. The different fractions of the middle class—advocates, physicians, merchants, farmers, artists—freely express among one another their discontent and their hatred, their ideas and their hopes. The Apennines, which form a barrier between them and the Pope, bring them nearer to Europe and liberty. I have never failed, after conversing with one of the middle class in the Legations, to inscribe in my tablets, *There is an Italian Nation!*

I travelled from Bologna to Florence with a young man whom I at first took, from the simple elegance of his dress, for an Englishman. But we fell so naturally into conversation, and my companion expressed himself so fluently in French, that I supposed him to be a fellow-countryman. When, however, I discovered how thoroughly he was versed in the state of the agriculture, manufactures, commerce, laws, the administration, and the politics of Italy, I could no longer doubt that he was an Italian and a Bolognese. What I chiefly admired in him was not so much the extent and variety of his knowledge, or the clearness and rectitude of his understanding, as the elevation of his character, and the moderation of his language. Every word he uttered was characterized by a profound sense of the dignity of his country, a bitter regret at the disesteem and neglect into which that country had fallen, and a firm hope in the justice of Europe in general and of one great prince in particular, and a certain combination of pride, melancholy, and sweetness which possessed an irresistible attraction for me. He nourished no hatred either against the Pope or any other person; he admitted the system of the priests, although utterly intolerable to the country, to be perfectly logical in itself. His dream was not of vengeance, but deliverance.

I learnt, some time afterwards, that my delightful travelling companion was a man of the *mezzo ceto*, and that there are many more such as he in Bologna.

But already had I inscribed in my tablets these words, thrice repeated, dated from the Court of the Posts, Piazza del Gran' Duca, Florence :—

" *There is an Italian Nation! There is an Italian Nation! There is an Italian Nation!* "

CHAPTER VII.

THE NOBILITY.

An Italian has said with pungent irony, "Who knows but that one of these days a powerful microscope may detect globules of nobility in the blood?"

I am too national not to applaud a good joke, and yet I must confess these "globules of nobility" do not positively offend my reason.

There is no doubt that sons take after their fathers. The Barons of the Middle Ages transmitted to their children a heritage of heroic qualities. Frederick the Great obtained a race of gigantic grenadiers by marrying men of six feet to women of five feet six. The children of a clever man are not fools, provided their mother has not failed in her duties; and when the Crétins of the Alps intermarry, they produce Crétins. We know dogs are slow or fast, keen-scented or keen-sighted, according to their breed, and we buy a two-year-old colt upon the strength of his pedigree. Can we consistently admit nobility among horses and dogs, and deny it among men?

Add to this, that the pride of bearing an illustrious name is a powerful incentive to well-doing. Noblemen have duties to fulfil both towards their ancestors and their posterity. They must walk uprightly under the penalty of dishonouring an entire race. Tradition obliges them to follow a path of honour and virtue, from which they cannot stray a single step without falling. They never sign their names without some elevated thought of an hereditary obligation.

I must admit that everything degenerates in the end, and that the purest blood may occasionally lose its high qualities, as the most generous wine turns to molasses or vinegar. But we have all of us met in the world a young man of loftier and prouder bearing, more high-minded and more courageous, than his fellows; or a woman so beautiful and simple and chaste, that she seemed made of a finer clay than the rest of her sex. We may be sure that both one and the other have in their blood some globules of nobility.

These precious globules, which no microscope will ever be powerful enough to detect, but which the intelligent observer sees with the naked eye, are rare enough in Europe, and I am not aware of their existence out of it. A small collection of them might be brought together in France, in Spain, in England, in Russia, in Germany, in Italy. Rome is one of the cities in which the fewest would be found. And yet the Roman nobility is surrounded with a certain prestige.

Thirty-one princes or dukes; a great number of marquises, counts, barons, and knights; a multitude of noble families without titles, sixty of whom were inscribed in the Capitol by Benedict XIV.; a vast extent of signiorial domains; a thousand palaces; a hundred picture-galleries, large and small; a considerable revenue; a prodigal display of horses, carriages, servants, and armorial bearings; some almost royal entertainments in the course of every winter; the remains of feudal privileges; and the respect of the lower orders: such are the more remarkable features which distinguish the Roman nobility, and expose it to the admiration of all the travelling cockneys of the universe.

Ignorance, idleness, vanity, servility, and above all incapacity; these are the pet vices which place it below all the aristocracies in Europe. Should I meet with any exceptions on my road, I shall consider it my duty to point them out.

The roots of the Roman nobility are very diverse. The Orsini and the Colonna families descend from the heroes or brigands of the Middle Ages. That of Caetani dates from 730. The houses of Massimo, Santa-Croce, and Muti, go back to Livy in search of their founders. Prince Massimo bears in his shield the trace of the marchings and countermarchings of Fabius Maximus, otherwise called Cunctator. His motto is, *Cunctando restituit.* Santa-Croce boasts of being an offshoot of Valerius Publicola. The Muti family counts Mutius Scævola among its ancestors. This nobility, whether authentic or not, is at all events very ancient, and is of independent origin. It has not been hatched under the robes of the Popes.

The second category is of Pontifical origin. Its titles and fortunes have their origin in nepotism. In the course of the seventeenth century, Paul V., Urban VIII.; Innocent X., Alexander VII., Clement IX., and Innocent XI. created the houses of Borghese, Barberini, Pamphili, Chigi, Rospigliosi, and Odescalchi. They vied with one another in aggrandising their humble families. The domains of the Borghese house, which make a tolerably large spot on the map of Europe, testify that Paul V. was by no means an unnatural uncle. The Popes have kept up the practice of ennobling their relations, but the scandal of their liberalities ceases with Pius VI., another of the Braschi family (1775–1800).

The last batch includes the bankers, such as Torlonia and Ruspoli, monopolists like Antonelli, millers like the

Macchi, bakers like the Dukes Grazioli, tobacconists like the Marchese Ferraiuoli, and farmers like the Marchese Calabrini.

I add, by way of memorandum, strangers, noble or not, as may be, who purchase an estate, get a title thrown into the bargain. A short time ago a French petty country gentleman, who had a little money, woke up a Roman Prince one fine morning, the equal of the Dorias, Torlonias, and of the baker Duke Grazioli.

For they are all equal from the hour when the Holy Father has signed their parchments. Whatever be the origin of their nobility and the antiquity of their houses, they go arm in arm, without any disputes as to precedence. The names of Orsini, Colonna, and Sforza, are jumbled together in the family of a former *domestique de place.* The son of a baker marries the daughter of a Lante de La Rovère, granddaughter of a Prince Colonna, and a Princess of Savoie-Carignan. There is no fear that the famous quarrel of the princes and dukes, which so roused the indignation of our stately St. Simon, will ever be repeated among the Roman aristocracy.

To what purpose should it be, gracious Heavens! Don't they well know—dukes and princes—that they are all alike inferior to the shabbiest of the cardinals? The day that a Capuchin receives the red hat, he acquires the right to splash the mud in their faces as he rides past in his gilded coach.

In all monarchical States, the king is the natural head of the nobility. The strongest term that a gentleman can make use of, in alluding to his house, is that it is as noble as the King. *As noble as the Pope* would be simply ludicrous, since a swineherd, the son of a swineherd, may be elected Pope, and receive the oath of fidelity from all the

Roman princes. They may well then consider themselves upon an equality among themselves, these poor grandees, seeing that they are equally looked down upon by a few priests.

They console themselves with the thought that they are superior to all the laymen in the world. This soothing vanity, neither noisy nor insolent, but none the less firmly rooted in their hearts, enables them to swallow the daily affront of conscious inferiority.

I am quite aware of the points in which they are inferior to the upstarts of the Church, but their affected superiority to other men is less evident to me.

As to their courage. Some years have elapsed since they had the opportunity of proving it on the field of battle.*

* A few of them did good service in the cause of liberty, and deserved well of their country, in the glorious but unsuccessful struggle of 1848, soon about to be renewed, and, let us hope, under happier auspices, and with a very different result.

Duke Filippo Lante Montefeltro, Colonel in command of a *corps d' armée* of the Roman Volunteers, occupied and held Treviso, whereby he at once assured the retreat of the Roman army, after its defeat at Cornuda on the 9th of May, 1848, by General Nugent, and prevented the advance of the Austrians upon Venice. The President Manin acknowledged that by his courage and patriotism he had saved Venice, and immediately sent him the commission of a full General. On the 16th of May, General Nugent arrived before Treviso with 16,000 men, and siege artillery. He at once summoned the place to surrender, giving General Lante till noon on the following day for consideration. At four the same evening, Lante sent for reply, "Come this evening. I shall expect you at six. We are here to fight, not to surrender!" After threatening the town for some days, Nugent retired from before it, and joined Radetzky.

Duke Bonelli, Captain of Dragoons, was Orderly Officer to General Durando at the capitulation of Vicenza.

Prince Bartolomeo Ruspoli served as a *private soldier* in the Roman

Heaven forbids duelling. The Government inculcates the gentler virtues.

They are not wanting in a certain ostentatious and theatrical liberality. A Piombino sent his ambassador to the conference at Vienna, allowing £4,000 for the expenses of the mission. A Borghese gave the mob of Rome a banquet that cost £48,000, to celebrate the return of Pius VII. Almost all the Roman princes open their palaces, villas, and galleries to the public. To be sure, old Sciarra used to sell permission to copy his pictures, but he was a notorious miser, and has found no imitators.

They practise generally the virtue of charity, in a somewhat indiscriminate manner, from the love of patronage, from pride, habit, and weakness, because they are ashamed to refuse. They are by no means badly disposed, they are good— I stop at this word, lest I should go too far.

They are not wanting in sense or intelligence. Prince Massimo is quoted for his good sense, and the two Caetani for their puns. Santa-Croce, though a little cracked, is no ordinary man. But what a wretched education the Gov-

Legion; he was one of the three Commissioners who were sent to the camp of Radetzky to treat for the capitulation of Vicenza.

Count Antonio Marescotti commanded the 1st Roman regiment of Grenadiers.

Count Bandini, son of a Princess Giustiniani, was also Orderly Officer to Durando.

Count Pianciani commanded the 3d regiment of Roman Volunteers.

Don Ludovico Lante (a younger brother of Filippo) was Captain in the 1st regiment of Roman Volunteers.

Adriano Borgia quitted the Pope's *Guardia Nobile* for a Colonelcy of Dragoons, in the service of the Roman Republic: he was an excellent officer.

Marquis Steffanoni commanded a company of young students.—TRANSL.

ernment gives them! When they are not the children, they are the pupils of priests, whose system principally consists in teaching them nothing. Get hold of a student of St. Sulpice, wash him tolerably clean, have him dressed by Alfred or Poole, and bejewelled by Castellani or Hunt and Roskel, let him learn to thrum a guitar, and sit upon a horse, and you'll have a Roman prince as good as the best of them.

You probably think it natural that people brought up at Rome, in the midst of the finest works of art in the world, should take a little interest in art, and know something about it. Pray be undeceived. This man has never entered the Vatican except to pay visits; that one knows nothing of his own gallery, but through the report of his house-steward. Another had never visited the Catacombs till he became Pope. They profess an elegant ignorance, which they think in good taste, and which will always be fashionable in a Catholic country.

I have said enough about the heart, mind, and education of the Roman nobility. A few words as to the fortunes of which they dispose.

I have before me a list which I believe to be authentic, as I copied it myself in a sure quarter. It comprises the net available incomes of the principal Roman families. I extract the most important:—

Corsini	£20,000
Borghese	18,000
Ludovisi	14,000
Grazioli	14,000
Doria	13,000
Rospigliosi	10,000
Colonna	8,000

Odescalchi	8,000
Massimo	8,000
Patrizi	6,000
Orsini	4,000
Strozzi	4,000
Torlonia	Unlimited.
Antonelli	Ditto.

It is not to be supposed that Grazioli, for instance, has himself alone nearly as large a gross income as Prince Borghese and his two brothers Aldobrandini and Salviati together. But the fact is that all the more ancient families are burdened with heavy hereditary charges, which enormously reduce their incomes. They are obliged to keep up chapels, churches, hospitals, and whole chapters of fat canons, while the nobles of yesterday are not called upon to pay for either the fame or the sins of their ancestors.

At all events the foregoing list proves the mediocrity as to wealth, as in everything else, of the Roman nobility. Not only are they unable to compete with the hard-working middle classes of London, Bâle, or Amsterdam, but they are infinitely less wealthy than the nobility of Russia or of England.

Is this because, as with us in France, an equitable law is constantly subdividing large properties? No. The law of primogeniture is in full vigour in the kingdom of the Pope, like every other abuse of the good old times. They provide for their younger sons as they can, and for their daughters as they please. It is not parental justice that ruins families. I have even heard it said that the elder brother is not obliged to put on mourning when the younger dies; which is a clear saving of so much black cloth.

This being the case, why are not the Roman princes

richer than they are? It is to be accounted for by two excellent reasons,—the love of show, and bad management.

Ostentation, the Roman disease, requires that every nobleman should have a palace in the city, and a palace in the country: carriages, horses, lacqueys and liveries. They can do without mattresses, linen, and armchairs, but a gallery of pictures is indispensable. It is not thought necessary to have a decent dinner every Sunday, but it is to have a terraced garden for the admiration of foreigners. These imaginary wants swallow up the income, and not unfrequently eat into the capital.

And yet I could point out half-a-dozen estates which could suffice for the prodigalities of a sovereign, if they were managed in the English, or even in the French fashion,—if the owner were to interfere personally, and see with his own eyes, instead of allowing a host of middlemen to come between him and his property, who of course enrich themselves at his expense.

Not that the Roman princes knowingly allow their affairs to go to ruin. They must by no means be confounded with the *grands seigneurs* of old France, who laughed over the wreck of their fortunes, and avenged themselves upon a steward by a *bon mot* and a kick. The Roman prince has an office, with shelves, desks, and clerks, and devotes some hours a day to business, examining accounts, poring over parchments, and signing papers. But being at once incapable and uneducated, his zeal serves but to liberate the rogues about him from responsibility. I heard of a nobleman who had inherited an enormous fortune, who condemned himself to the labor of a clerk at £50 a year, who remained faithful to his desk even to extreme old age, and who, thanks to some blunder or other in management, died insolvent.

Pity them if you please, but cast not the stone at them.

They are such as education has made them. Look at those brats of various ages from six to ten, walking along the Corso in double file, between a couple of Jesuits. They are embryo Roman nobles. Handsome as little Cupids, in spite of their black coats and white neckcloths, they will all grow up alike, under the shadow of their pedagogue's broad-brimmed hat.

Already are their minds like a well-raked garden, from which ideas have been carefully rooted out. Their hearts are purged alike of good and evil passions. Poor little wretches, they will not even have any vices.

As soon as they shall have passed their last examinations, and obtained their diplomas of ignorance, they will be dressed in the latest London fashions, and be turned out into the public promenades. They will pace for ever the pavement of the Corso, they will wear out the alleys of the Pincian Hill, the Villa Borghese, and the Villa Pamphili. They will ride, drive, and walk about, armed with a whip, eye-glass, or cane, as may be, until they are made to marry. Regular at Mass, assiduous at the theatre, you may see them smile, gape, applaud, make the sign of the cross, with an equal absence of emotion. They are almost all inscribed on the list of some religious fraternity or other. They belong to no club, play timidly, rarely make a parade of social irregularities, drink without enthusiasm, and never ruin themselves by horse-racing. In short, their general conduct is beyond all praise; and the life of dolls made to say "Papa!" and "Mama!" is equally irreproachable.

One fine day they attain their twenty-fifth year. At this age, an American has already tried his hand at a dozen trades, made four fortunes, and at least one bankruptcy, has gone through a couple of campaigns, had a lawsuit, established a new religious sect, killed half-a-dozen men with his revolver, freed a negress, and conquered an island. An Englishman has passed some stiff examinations, been attached to an embassy, founded a factory, converted a Catholic, gone round the world, and read the complete works of Walter Scott. A Frenchman has rhymed a tragedy, written for two newspapers, been wounded in three duels, twice attempted suicide, vexed fourteen husbands, and changed his politics nineteen times. A German has slashed fifteen of his dearest friends, swallowed sixty hogsheads of beer and the Philosophy of Hegel, sung eleven thousand couplets, compromised a tavern waiting-maid, smoked a million of pipes, and been mixed up with, at least, two revolutions.

The Roman prince has done nothing, seen nothing, learnt nothing, loved nothing, suffered nothing. His parents or guardians open a cloister gate, take out a young girl as inexperienced as himself, and the pair of innocents are bidden to kneel before a priest, who gives them permission to become parents of another generation of innocents like themselves.

Probably you expect to find them living unhappily together. Not at all. And yet the wife is pretty. The monotonous routine of her convent education has not so frozen her heart that she is incapable of loving; her uncultivated mind will spontaneously develope itself when it comes in contact with the world. She will not fail, ere long, to discover the inferiority of her husband. The more her education has been neglected, the greater is her chance of remaining womanly, that is to say, intelligent, tender, and charming. In truth, the harmony of their household is less likely to be disturbed at Rome than it would be at Paris or Vienna.

Yes, the huge extinguisher which Heaven holds suspended over the city of Rome, stifles even the subtle spark of passion. If Vesuvius were here, it would have been cold for the last forty years. The Roman princesses were not a little talked of up to the end of the thirteenth century. Under the French rule their gallantry assumed a military complexion. They used to go and see their admirers play billiards at the Cafè Nuovo. But hypocrisy and morality have made immense progress since the restoration. The few who have afforded matter for the scandalous chronicles of Rome are sexagenarians, and their adventures are inscribed on the tablets of history, between Austerlitz and Waterloo.

The young princess whom we have just seen entering upon her married life, will begin by presenting her husband with sundry little princes and princesses; and there is no rampart against illicit affection like your row of little cradles.

In five or six years, when she might have leisure for evil thoughts, she will be bound hand and foot by the exigencies of society. You shall have a specimen of the mode in which she spends her days during the winter season. Her morning is devoted to dressing, breakfasting, her children, and her husband. From one to three she returns the visits she has received, in the exact form in which they were paid to her. The first act of politeness is to go and see your acquaintance; the second, to leave your card in person; the third, to send the same bit of pasteboard by a servant *ad hoc*. At three, all the world drives to the Villa Borghese, where there is a general salutation of acquaintances with the tips of the fingers. At four, up the Pincio. At five, it files backwards and forwards along the Corso. Everybody who is anybody is condemned to this triple promenade. If a single woman —who is anybody—were to absent herself, it would be inferred, as a matter of course, that she was ill, and a general inquiry as to the nature of her complaint would be instituted.

At close of day all go home. After dinner another toilette, and out for the evening. Every house has its particular reception-night. And a pure and simple reception indeed it is, without play, without music, without conversation; a mere interchange of bows and curtsies, and cold commonplaces. At rare intervals a ball breaks the ice, and shakes off the *ennui* generated by this system. Poor women! In an existence at once so busy and so void, there is not even room for friendship. Two who may have been friends from childhood, brought up in the same convent, married into the same world, may meet one another daily and at all hours, and yet may not be able to enjoy ten minutes of intimate conversation in the whole year. The brightest, the best, is known but by her name, her title, and her fortune. Judgments are passed on her beauty, her toilet, and her diamonds, but nobody has the opportunity or the leisure to penetrate into the depths of her mind. A really distinguished woman once said to me, "I feel that I become stupid when I enter these drawing-rooms. Vacancy seizes me at the very threshold." Another, who had lived in France, regretted, with tears, the absence of those charming friendships, so cheerful and so cordial, that exist between the young married women of Paris.

When the Carnival arrives, it mingles everything without uniting anything. In truth, one is never more solitary than in the midst of noise and crowds. Then comes Lent; and then the grand comedy of Easter; and after that the family departs for the country, which means, economizing for some months in a huge half-furnished mansion. In short, the romance of a Roman Princess is made up of a certain number of noisy winters, and dull summers, and plenty of children. If there be, by chance, any more exciting chapters, they are doubtless known to the confessor.

"Ce ne sont pas là mes affaires."

You must go far from Rome to find any real nobility. Here and there in the Mediterranean provinces some fallen family may be met with, living poorly upon the produce of a small estate, and still looked up to with a certain respect by its wealthier neighbours. The lower orders respect it because it has been something once, and even because it is nothing under the present hated government. These little provincial aristocrats, ignorant, simple, and proud, are a sort of relic of the Middle Ages left behind in the middle of the nineteenth century. I only mention them to recall the fact of their existence.

But if you will accompany me over the Apennines, into the glorious cities of the Romagna, I can show you more than one nobleman of great name and ancient lineage, who cultivates at once his lands and his intellect; who knows all that we know; who believes all that we believe, and nothing more; who takes an active interest in the misfortunes of Italy, and who, looking to free and happy Europe, hopes, through the sympathy of nations and the justice of sovereigns, to obtain the deliverance of his country. I met in certain palaces at Bologna a brilliant writer, applauded on every stage in Italy; a learned economist, quoted in the most serious reviews throughout Europe; a controversialist, dreaded by the priests; and all these individualities united in the single person of a Marquis of thirty-four, who may, perhaps, one of these days play an important part in the Italian revolution.

CHAPTER VIII.

FOREIGNERS.

Permit me to open this chapter by recalling some recollections of the golden age.

A century or two ago, when old aristocracies, old royalties, and old religions imagined themselves eternal; when Popes innocently assured the fortunes of their nephews, and the welfare of their mistresses; when the simplicity of Catholic countries regilt annually the pontifical idol; when Europe contained some half-million of individuals who deemed themselves created for mutual understanding and amusement, without any thought of the classes beneath them, Rome was the Paradise of foreigners, and foreigners were the Providence of Rome.

A gentleman of birth took it into his head to visit Italy, for the sake of kissing the Pope's toe, and perhaps other local curiosities. He managed to have a couple of years of leisure,—put three letters of introduction into one pocket, and 50,000 crowns into the other, and stepped into his travelling carriage.

In those days people did not go to Rome to spend a week there and away again; for it was a month or two's journey from France. The crack of the postilions' whips used to announce to the Eternal City in general the arrival of a distinguished guest. *Domestiques de place* flocked to the call. The luckiest of them took possession of the new comer by entering his service. In a few days he provided his master with a palace, furniture, footmen, carriages, and horses. The foreigner settled himself comfortably, and then presented his letters of introduction. His credentials being examined, the best society at once oppened its arms to him, and cried, "You are one of us!" From that moment he was at home wherever he went. He was a guest at every house. He danced, supped, played, and made love to the ladies. And of course, in his turn, he opened his own palace to his liberal entertainers, adding a new feature to the brilliancy of a Roman winter.

No foreigner failed to carry away with him some recollection of a city so fertile in marvels. One bought pictures, another ancient marbles, this one medals, that one books. The trade of Rome prospered by this circulation of foreign money.

The heats of summer drove away foreigners as well as natives; but they never went far. Naples, Florence, or Venice offered them agreeable quarters till the return of the winter season. And they had excellent reasons for returning to Rome, which is the only city in the world in which one has never seen everything. Some of them so entirely forgot their own countries, that death overtook them between the Piazza del Popolo and the Piazza de Venizia. If any exiled themselves to their native land, they did it in sheer self-defence, when their pockets were empty. Rome bade them a tender adieu, piously keeping their likeness in its memory and their money in its coffers.

The Revolution of 1793 somewhat disturbed this agreeable order of things; but it was a mere storm between two fine summer days. Neither the Roman aristocracy, nor its constant troop of guests, took this brutal overthrow of their elegant pleasures in earnest. The exile of the Pope, the French occupation, and many similar accidents, were supported with a noble resignation, and forgotten with the readiness of good taste. 1815 passed a sponge over some years of very foul history. All the inscriptions which recalled the glory or the beneficence of France were conscientiously erased. It was even proposed to do away with the lighting of the streets, not only because they threw too strong a light upon certain nocturnal matters, but because they dated from the time of Miollis and De Tournon. Even now, in 1859, the fleur-de-lis points out what is French property. A marble table in the church of San Luigi dei Francesi promises indulgence to those who will pray for the king of France. The French convent of the Trinità dei Monti—that worthy claustral establishment which sold us the picture of Daniel di Volterra and then took it back—possesses the portraits of all the kings of France, from Pharamond to Charles X. There you see Louis XVII. between Louis XVI. and Louis XVIII.; but in this historical gallery there is no more mention of Napoleon or of Louis-Philippe, than of Nana-Sahib or Marat.

A city so respectful to the past, so faithful to the worship of bygone recollections, is the natural asylum of sovereigns fallen from their thrones. It is to Rome that they come to foment their contusions, and to heal the wounds of their pride. They live there agreeably, surrounded by the few followers who have remained faithful to them. A miniature court, assembled in their antechamber, crowns them in private, hails them on rising with epithets of royalty, and pours forth incense in their dressing-room. The Roman nobility, and foreigners of distinction, live with them in an unequal intimacy, humbling themselves in order that they may be raised; and sowing a great deal of veneration to reap a very light crop of familiarity. The Pope and his Cardinals, upon principle, are lavish of attentions which they would perhaps refuse them on the throne. In short, the king who has been the most battered and shaken by his fall, and the most ill-used by his ungrateful subjects, has but to take refuge in Rome, and by the double aid of a vivid imagination and a well-filled purse, he may persuade himself that he is still reigning over an absent people.

The reverses of royalty which ended the eighteenth and commenced the nineteenth centuries, sent to Rome a colony of crowned heads. The modifications which European society has undergone have more recently brought many less illustrious guests, not even members of the aristocracy of their own country. It is certain that for the last fifty years, wealth, education, and talent have shared the rights formerly belonging to birth alone. Rome has seen foreigners arriving in travelling carriages who were not born great,—distinguished artists, eminent writers, diplomatists sprung from the people, tradesmen elevated to the rank of capitalists, men of the world who are in their place everywhere, because everywhere they know how to live. The best society did not receive them without submitting them to careful inquiry, in order to ascertain that they brought no dangerous doctrines; and then it seemed to say to them: "You cannot be our relations—be our masonic brothers!"

I have said that the Roman princes are, if not without pride, at least without arrogance. This observation extends to the princes of the Church. They welcome a foreigner of modest condition, provided he speaks and thinks like themselves upon two or three capital questions, has a profound veneration for certain time-honoured lumber, and curses heartly certain innovations. You must show them the white paw of the fable, if you wish them to open their doors to you.

On this point they are immovable. They will not listen

to rank, to fortune, or even to the most imperious political necessities. If France were to send them an ambassador who failed to show them the white paw, the ambassador of France would not get inside the doors of the aristocratic *salons*. If Horace Vernet were named director of the Academy, neither his name nor his office would open to him certain houses where he was received as a friend previously to 1830. And why? Because Horace Vernet was one of the public men of the Revolution of July.

Do not imagine, however, that paying respect to Cardinals involves paying respect to religion, or that it is necessary to attend Mass in order to get invited to balls. What is absolutely indispensable is, to believe that everything at Rome is good, to regard the Papacy as an arch, the Cardinals as so many saints, abuses as principles, and to applaud the march of the Government, even though it stand still. It is considered good taste to praise the virtues of the lower orders, their simple faith, and their indifference as to political affairs, and to despise that middle-class which is destined to bring about the next revolution.

I conversed much with some of the foreigners who live in Rome, and who mix with its best society. One of the most distinguished and the most agreeable of them often gave me advice which, though I have not followed, I have not forgotten.

"My dear friend," he used to say, "I know but two ways of writing about Rome. You must choose for yourself. If you declaim against the priestly government, its abuses, vices, and injustice; against the assassinations, the uncultivated lands, the bad air, the filthiness of the streets; against the many scandals, the hypocrisies, the robberies, the lotteries, the Ghetto, and all that follows as a matter of course, you will earn the somewhat barren honour of having added the thousand and first pamphlet to those which have appeared since the time of Luther. All has been said that can be said against the Popes. A man who pretends to originality should not lend his voice to the chorus of brawling reformers. Remember, too, that the Government of this country, though very mild and very paternal, never forgives! Even if it wished to do so, it cannot. It must defend its principle, which is sacred. Don't close the gates of Rome against yourself. You will be so glad to revisit it, and we shall be so happy to receive you again! If you wish to support a new and original theme, and to gain fame which will not be wholly unprofitable, dare to declare boldly that everything is good—even that which all agree to pronounce bad. Praise without restriction an order of things which has been solidly maintained for eighteen centuries. Prove that everything here is firmly established, and that the network of pontifical institutions is linked together by a powerful logic. Bravely resist those aspirations after reform which may haply urge you to demand such and such changes. Remember that you cannot disturb old constitutions with impunity; that the displacement of a single stone may bring down the whole edifice. How do you know, that the particular abuse which most offends you is not absolutely necessary to the very existence of Rome? Good and evil mixed together form a cement more durable than the elaborately selected materials of which modern utopias are made. I who tell you this have been here many years, and am quite comfortable and contented. Whither should I go if Rome were to be turned topsy-turvy? Where should we establish our dethroned sovereigns? Where would a home be found for Roman Catholic worship? You have no doubt been told that some people are dissatisfied with the administration: but what of that? They are not of *our* world. You never meet them in the good society you frequent. If the demands of the middle class were to be complied with, everything would be overturned. Have you any wish to see manufactories erected round St. Peter's and turnipfields about the fountain of Egeria? These native shopkeepers seem to imagine the country belongs to them because they happen to be born in it. Can one conceive a more ridiculous pretension? Let them know that Rome is the property in copartnership of people of birth, of people of taste, and of artists. It is a museum confided to the guardianship of the Holy Father; a museum of old monuments, old pictures, and old institutions. Let all the rest of the world change, but build me a Chinese wall round the Papal States, and never let the sound of the railway-whistle be heard within its sacred precincts! Let us preserve for admiring posterity at least one magnificent specimen of absolute power, ancient art, and the Roman Catholic religion!"

This is the language of foreign inhabitants of Rome of the old stamp,—estimable people, and sincere believers, who have gone on year after year witnessing the ceremonies of St. Peter's, and the *Fête des Oignons* in the St. John Lateran, till they have acquired an ecclesiastical turn of thought and expression, a habit of seeing things through the spectacles of the Sacred College, and a faith which has no sympathy with the outer world. I do not share their opinions, and I have never found their advice particularly useful; but they interest me, I like them, and I sincerely pity them. Who can tell what events they are destined to witness in their time? Who can foresee the spectacles which the future reserves for them, and the changes that their habits will be made to undergo by the Italian revolution? Already their hearing is distracted by the locomotives that rush between Rome and Frascati; already the shriek of the steam-blast daily and nightly hisses insolently at the respectable comedy of the past between Rome and Civita Vecchia. Steamboats, another engine of disorder, furnish the bi-weekly means of an invasion of the most dangerous character. Those dozens of travellers who throng the streets and the squares are about as much like our good old foreign tourists, as the barbarians of Attila were like the worthy Spaniard who came to Rome on purpose to see Titus Livius.

Examine them carefully; they are of every possible condition; for now that travelling costs next to nothing, everybody is able to afford himself a sight of Rome. Briefless barristers, physicians without practice, office-clerks, poor students, apprentices, and shop-boys drop down like hail on the Eternal City, for the sake of saying that they have taken the Communion in it. The Holy Week brings every year a swarm of these locusts. Their entire *impedimenta* consist of a carpet-bag and an umbrella, and of course they put up at a hotel. In fact hotels have been built on purpose to receive them. When everybody hired houses, there was no need of hotels. The 'Minerva' is the type of the modern Roman caravansary. Your bed is charged half-a-crown per night; you dine in a refectory with a traveller at each elbow. The character of the travelling class which invades Rome about Easter is illustrated by the conversation which you hear going on around you at the *table d'hôte* of the 'Minerva.' The following is a specimen:—

One says triumphantly, "I have *done* two museums, three galleries, and four ruins, to-day."

"I stuck to the churches," says another, "I had floored seventeen by one o'clock."

"The deuce you had! You keep the game alive."

"Yes, I want to have a whole day left for the suburbs."

"Oh, burn the suburbs! I've got no time to see them.

If I have a day to spare, I must devote it to *buying chaplets*." *

"I suppose you've seen the Villa Borghese?"

"Oh yes, I consider that in the city, although it is in fact outside the walls."

"How much did they charge you for going over it?"

"A paul."

"I paid two—I've been robbed."

"As for that, they're all robbers."

"You're right, but the sight of Rome is worth all it costs."

Shades of the travellers of the olden time—delicate, subtle, genial spirits—what think you of conversations such as this? Surely you must opine that your footmen knew Rome better, and talked more to the purpose about it.

Across the table I hear a citizen of London town narrating to a curious audience how he has to-day seen the two great lions of Rome,—the Coliseum, and Cardinal Antonelli. The conclusion he arrives at is, that the first is a very fine ruin, and the second a very clever man.

A provincial dowager of the devotee class, is worth listening to. She has toiled through the entire ceremonies of the Holy Week. She has knelt close to the Pope, and declares his mode of giving the Benediction the most sublime thing on earth. The good lady has spared neither time nor money in order to carry home a choice collection of *relics*. Among other objects of adoration she has a bone of St. Perpetua, and a real bit of the real Cross. Not satisfied with these, she is bent on obtaining the Pope's palm-branch, the very identical palm-branch which his Holiness has carried in

* The ordinary British tourist must not look for his portrait in the witty Author's picture. It is clear that here and elsewhere the pilgrims are all assumed to be true sons of *the* Church.—Transl.

his own sacred hand. This is with her a fixed idea, a positive question of salvation. The poor old soul has not the smallest doubt, that this bit of stick will open for her the gates of Paradise. She has made her request to a priest, who will transmit it to a Monsignore, who will forward it to a Cardinal. Her importunity and her simplicity will, doubtless, move somebody. She will get the precious bough, and she is convinced that when she arrives at home with it, all the devotees in the province will burst with envy.

Among these batches of ridiculous travellers, you are certain to find some ecclesiastics. Here is one from our own country. You have known him in France. Does not he strike you as being somewhat changed? Not in his looks, but his manner. Beneath the shadow of his own church tower, in the midst of his own flock, he used to be the mildest, the meekest, and most modest of parish priests. He bowed low to the Mayor, and to the most microscopic of the authorities. At Rome, his hat seems glued to his head. I almost think—Heaven forgive me!—it is a trifle cocked. How jauntily his cassock is tucked up! How he struts along the street! Is not his hand on his hip? Something very like it. The reason of this change is as clear as the sun at noon. He is in a kingdom governed by his own class. He inhales an atmosphere impregnated with clerical pride and theocratic omnipotence. Phiz! It is a bottle of champagne saluting him with the cork. By the time he has drunk all the contents of the intoxicating beverage, he will begin to mutter between his teeth that the French clergy does not get its deserts, and that we are a long time in restoring to it the property taken away by the Revolution.

I actually heard this argument maintained on board the steamer which brought me back to France. The principal passengers were Prince Souworf, Governor of the province of Riga, one of the most distinguished men in Europe; M. de la Rochefoucauld, attached to the French embassy; M. de Angelis, a highly educated and really distinguished *mercante di campagna;* M. Oudry, engineer of the Civita Vecchia railway: and a French ecclesiastic of a respectable age and corpulence. This reverend personage, who was nowise disinclined to argumentation, and who had just left a country where the priests are never wrong, took to holding-forth after dinner upon the merits of the Pontifical Government. I answered as well as I could, like a man unaccustomed to public speaking. Driven to my last entrenchments, and called upon to relate some fact which should not redound to the Pope's credit, I chose, at hazard, a recent event then known to all Rome, as it was speedily about to be to all Europe. My honourable interlocutor met my statement with the most unqualified, formal, and unhesitating denial. He accused me of impudently calumniating an innocent administration, and of propagating lies fabricated by the enemies of religion. His language was so sublimely authoritative, that I felt confounded, overpowered, crushed, and, for a moment, I asked myself whether I had not really been telling a lie.

The story I had related was that of the boy Mortara.

But I return to Rome and our travellers in the trumpery line. Those we overheard before are already gone. But their places have been quickly filled. They follow one another, like vapours rising from the ocean, and they are as much like one another as one sea-wave is to its predecessor. See them laying-in their stocks of Roman *souvenirs* at the shops in the Corso and the Via Condotti. Their selections are principally from the cheap rosaries, coarse mosaics, and gilt jewellery, and generally those articles of which a lot may be had for a crown-piece. They care little for what is really good in its way; all they want is something which can be bought nowhere but at Rome, and which will serve to their descendants as the evidence of their visit to the Eternal City. They haggle as if they were at market, and yet, when they get back to the 'Minerva,' they wonder they have so little to show for their money.

If they took home nothing worse than their cheap rosaries, I should not find fault with them; but they carry opinions and impressions. Don't tell them of the abuses which swarm throughout the kingdom of the Pope. They will bridle up, and answer that for their parts they never saw a single one. As the surface of things is smooth, at least in the best quarter of the town—the only quarter these good folks are likely to have seen—they assume, as a matter of course, that all is well. They have seen the Pope and the Cardinals in all their glory and all their innocence at the Sistine Chapel; and of course it is not on Easter Sunday, and in the eyes of the whole multitude, that Cardinal Antonelli occupies himself with his business or his pleasures. When Monsignore B—— dishonoured a young girl, who died of the outrage, and then sent her affianced bridegroom to the galleys, he did not select the Sistine Chapel as the theatre of his exploits.

You must not attempt to extract pity for the Italian nation from these foreign pilgrims of the Holy Week. The honest souls have marked the uncultivated waste which extends from Civita Vecchia to Rome, and they have at once inferred that the people are idle. They have been importuned for alms by miserable-looking objects in the streets, and they conclude that the lower class is a class of beggars.

The cicerone who took them about, whispered some significant words in their ears, and they are persuaded that every Italian is in the habit of offering his wife or his daughter to foreigners. You would astonish these profound observers immeasurably, if you were to tell them that the Pope has three millions of subjects who in no way resemble the Roman rabble.

Thus it happens that the flying visitor, the superficial traveller, the communicant of the Holy Week, the guest of the 'Minerva,' is a ready-made foe to the nation, a natural defender of the clerical government.

As for the permanent foreign visitors, if they be men enervated by the climate or by pleasure, indifferent to the fate of nations, strangers to political chicane, they will, in the natural order of events, become converted to the ideas of the Roman aristocracy, between a quadrille and a cup of chocolate.

If they be studious men, or men of action, sent for a specific object, charged to unravel certain mysteries, or to support certain principles, their conversion will be undertaken in due form.

I have seen officers, bold, frank, off-hand men, nowise suspected of Jesuitism, who have allowed themselves to be gently carried away into the by-paths of reaction by an invisible influence, until they have been heard swearing, like pagans, against the enemies of the Pope. Even our own generals, less easy to be caught, are sometimes laid hold of. The Government cajoles them without loving them.

No effort is spared to persuade them that all is for the best. The Roman princes, who think themselves superior to all men, treat them upon a footing of perfect equality. The Cardinals caress them. These men in petticoats possess marvellous seductions, and are irresistible in the art of wheedling. The Holy Father himself converses now with one, now with the other, and addresses each as "My dear General!" A soldier must be very ungrateful, very badly taught, and have fallen off sadly from the old French chivalry, if he refuses to let himself be killed at the gates of the Vatican where his vanity has been so charmingly tickled.

Our ambassadors, too, are resident foreigners, exposed to the personal flatteries of Roman society. Poor Count de Rayneval! He was so petted, and cajoled, and deceived, that he ended by penning the NOTE of the 14th of May, 1856.

His successor, the Duke de Gramont, is not only an accomplished gentleman, but a man of talent, with a highly cultivated mind. The Emperor sent him from Turin to Rome, so it was to be expected that the Pontifical Government would appear to him doubly detestable, first, from its own defects, and then by comparison with what he had just quitted. I had the honour of conversing with this brilliant young diplomatist, shortly after his arrival, when the Roman people expected a great deal of him. I found him opposed to the ideas of the Count de Rayneval, and very far from disposed to countersign the *Note* of the 14th of May. Nevertheless, he was beginning to judge the administration of the Cardinals, and the grievances of the people, with something more than diplomatic impartiality. If I were to express what appeared to be his opinion, in common parlance, I should say he would have put the governors and the governed in a bag together. I would wager that, three months afterwards, the bag would contain none but the governed, and that he would think it only fit to be flung into the water. Such is the influence of ecclesiastical cajoleries over even the most gifted minds.

What can the Romans hope from our diplomacy, when they see one of the most notorious lacqueys of the Pontifical coterie lording it at the French Embassy? The name of the upright man I allude to is Lasagni; his business is that of a consistorial advocate; we pay him for deceiving us. He is known for a *Nero*,—that is, a fanatical reactionist. The secretaries of the embassy despise him, and yet are familiar with him; tell him they know he is going to lie, and yet listen to what he says. He smirks, bends double, pockets his money and laughs at us in his sleeve. Verily, friend Lasagni, you are quite right! But I regret the eighteenth century—there were then such things as canes.

CHAPTER IX.

ABSOLUTE CHARACTER OF THE TEMPORAL POWER OF THE POPE.

THE Counsellor de Brosses, who wished no harm to the Pope, wrote in 1740 :—" The Papal Government, although in fact the worst in Europe, is at the same time the mildest."

The Count de Tournon, an honest man, an excellent economist, a Conservative as to all existing powers, and a judge rather too much prejudiced in favour of the Popes, said, in 1832 :—" From this concentration of the powers of pontiff, bishop, and sovereign, naturally arises the most absolute authority possible over temporal affairs; but the exercise of this authority, tempered by the usages and forms of government, is even still more so by the virtues of the Pontiffs who for many years have filled the chair of St. Peter; so that this most absolute of governments is exercised with extreme mildness. The Pope is an elective sovereign; his States are the patrimony of Catholicism, because they are the pledge of the independence of the chief of the faithful, and the reigning Pope is the supreme administrator, the guardian of this domain."

Finally, the Count de Rayneval, the latest and least felicitous apologist of the Papacy, made in 1856 the following admissions :—" *Not long ago* the ancient traditions of the Court of Rome were faithfully observed. All modifications of established usages, all improvements, even material, were viewed with an evil eye, and seemed full of danger. Public affairs were exclusively managed by prelates. The higher posts in the State were by law interdicted to laymen. In practice the different powers were often confounded. The principle of pontifical infallibility was applied to administrative questions. The personal decision of the Sovereign had been known to reverse the decision of the tribunals, even in civil matters. The Cardinal Secretary of State, first minister in the fullest extent of the term, concentred in his own hands all the powers of the State. Under his supreme direction the different branches of the administration were confided to clerks rather than ministers. These neither formed a council, nor deliberated together upon the affairs of the State. The public finances were administered in the most profound secrecy. No information was communicated to the nation as to the mode in which its revenues were spent. Not only did the budget remain a mystery, but it was afterwards discovered that the accounts were frequently not made up and balanced. Lastly, municipal liberties, which are appreciated above all others by the Italians, and which more particularly respond to their real tendencies, had been submitted to the most restrictive measures. *But from the day on which Pope Pius IX. ascended the throne,*" etc. etc.

Thus we find that the *not long ago* of the Count de Rayneval is an exact date. It means, in good French, "before the election of Pius IX.," or again, "up to the 16th of June, 1846."

Thus also M. de Brosses, if he could have returned to Rome in 1846, would have found there, by the admission of the Count de Rayneval himself, the worst government in Europe.

And thus the most absolute of governments, as M. de Tournon calls it, still existed in Rome in 1846.

Up to the 16th of June, 1846, Catholicity owned the six millions of acres of which the Roman territory consists; the Pope was the administrator, the guardian, the steward; and the citizens of the State seem to have been the ploughmen.

Up to this era of deliverance, a systematic despotism had deprived the subjects of the Pope, not only of all participation in public affairs, but of the simplest and most legitimate liberties, of the most innocuous progress, and even—I shudder as I write it—of recourse to the laws. The whim of one man had arbitrarily reversed the decisions of the courts of law. And lastly, an incapable and disorderly caste had wasted the public finances without rendering an account to any one, occasionally even without rendering it to themselves. All these statements must be believed, because it is the Count de Rayneval who makes them.

Before proceeding, I maintain that this state of things, now admitted by the apologists of the Papacy, justifies all the discontent of the subjects of the Pope, all their complaints, all their recriminations, all their outbreaks previous to 1846.

But let me ask this question. Is it true that, since 1846, the Papal Government has ceased to be the worst in Europe?

If you can show me a worse, I will go and announce the discovery at Rome, and I rather fancy I shall considerably astonish the Romans.

Is the absolute authority of the Papacy limited in any way but by the individual virtues of the Pope? No.

Does the Constitution of 1848, or the *Motu Proprio* of 1849, set limits to this authority? No. The first has been torn up, the second never observed.

Has the Pope renounced his title of administrator, or irresponsible guardian of the patrimony of Catholicism? Never.

Is the management of public affairs exclusively in the hand of prelates? As much so as ever.

Are the higher posts in the State still by law interdicted to laymen? Not by law, but in fact they are.

Are the different powers still confounded in practice? More so than they ever were. The governors of cities act as judges, and the bishops as public administrators.

Has the Pope abandoned any portion of his infallibility as to worldly matters? None whatever.

Has he deprived himself of the right of overruling the decisions of the Courts of Appeal? No.

Has the Cardinal Secretary of State ceased to be a reigning Minister? He reigns as absolutely as ever; and the other ministers are more like footmen than clerks to him. They may be seen any morning waiting in his antechamber.

Is there a Council of Ministers? Yes, whereat the Ministers attend to receive the Cardinal's orders.

Are the public finances publicly administered? No.

Does the nation vote the taxes, or are they taken from the nation? The old system still exists.

Are municipal liberties at all extended? They were greater in 1816 than they are at present.

At the present day, as in the days of the most extreme pontifical despotism, the Pope is all in all; he has all; he can do all; he exercises a perpetual dictatorship, without control or limit.

I own no systematic aversion to the exceptional exercise of a dictatorship. The ancient Romans knew its value, often had recourse to it, and derived benefit from it. When the enemy was at the gates, and the Republic in danger, the

Senate and the people, usually so suspicious, placed all their rights in the hands of one man, and cried, "Save us!" Some grand dictatorships are to be found in the history of all times and all peoples. If we examine the different stages of humanity, we shall find almost at every one a dictator. One dictatorship created the unity of France, another its military greatness, and a third its prosperity in peace. Benefits so important as these, which nations cannot acquire alone, are well worth the temporary sacrifice of every liberty. A man of genius, who is at the same time an honest man, and who becomes invested with a boundless authority, is almost a God upon earth.

But the duties of the dictator are in exact proportion to the extent of his powers. A parliamentary sovereign, who walks in a narrow path traced out by two Chambers, and who hears discussed in the morning what he is to do in the evening, is almost innocent of the faults of his reign. On the contrary, the less a dictator is responsible for his actions by the terms of the Constitution, the more does he become so in the eyes of posterity. History will reproach him for the good he has failed to do, when he could do everything; and his omissions will be accounted to him for crimes.

I will add, that under no circumstances should the dictatorship last long. Not only would it be an absurdity to attempt to make it hereditary, but the man who should think of exercising it perpetually would be insane. A sick patient allows himself to be bound by the surgeon who is about to save his life; but when the operation is over he demands to be set at liberty. Nations act in a like manner. From the day when the benefits conferred by the master cease to compensate for the loss of liberty, the nation demands the restoration of its rights, and a wise dictator will comply with the demand.

I have often conversed in the Papal States with enlightened and honourable men, who rank as the heads of the middle class. They have said to me almost unanimously:—

"If a man were to drop down from Heaven among us with sufficient power to cut to the root of abuses, to reform the administration, to send the priests to church and the Austrians to Vienna, to promulgate a civil code, make the country healthy, restore the plains to cultivation, encourage manufactures, give freedom to commerce, construct railways, secularize education, propagate modern ideas, and put us into a condition to bear comparison with the most enlightened countries in Europe, we would fall at his feet, and obey him as we do God. You are told that we are ungovernable. Give us but a prince capable of governing, and you shall see whether we will haggle about the conditions of power! Be he who he may, and come he whence he may, he shall be absolutely free to do what he chooses, so long as there is anything to be done. All we ask is, that when his task is accomplished, he shall let us share the power with him. Rest assured that even then we shall give him good measure. The Italians are accommodating, and are not ungrateful. But ask us not to support this everlasting, do-nothing, tormenting, ruinous dictatorship, which a succession of decrepit old men transmit from one to another. Nor do they even exercise it themselves; but each in his turn, too weak to govern, hastens to shift a burden which overpowers him, and delivers us, bound hand and foot, to the worst of his Cardinals!"

It is too true that the Popes do not themselves exercise their absolute power. If the *White Pope*, or the Holy Father, governed personally, we might hope, with a little aid from the imagination, that a miracle of grace would make him walk straight. He is rarely very capable or very highly educated: but as the statue of the Commendatore said, "He who is enlightened by Heaven wants no other light." Unfortunately the *White Pope* transfers his political functions to a *Red Pope*, that is to say, an omnipotent and irresponsible Cardinal, under the name of a Secretary of State. This one man represents the sovereign within and without,—speaks for him, acts for him, replies to foreigners, commands his subjects, expresses the Pope's will, and not unfrequently imposes his own upon him.

This second-hand dictator has the best reasons in the world for abusing his power. If he could hope to succeed his master, and wear the crown in his turn, he might set an example, or make a show, of all the virtues. But it is impossible for a Secretary of State to be elected Pope. Not only is custom opposed to it, but human nature forbids it. Never will the Cardinals in conclave assembled agree among one another to crown the man who has ruled them all during a reign. Old Lambruschini had taken all his measures to secure his election. There were very few Cardinals who had not promised him their voices, and yet it was Pius IX. who ascended the throne. The illustrious Consalvi, one of the great statesmen of our age, made the same attempt with as little success. After such instances it is clear that Cardinal Antonelli has no chance of attaining the tiara; and therefore no interest in doing good.

If he could at least hope that the successor of Pius IX. would retain him in his functions, he might observe a little caution. But it has never yet happened that the same Secretary of State has reigned under two Popes. Such an event never will occur, because it never has occurred. We are in a land where the future is the very humble servant of the past. Tradition absolutely requires that a new Pope should disgrace the favourite of his predecessor, by way of initiating his Papacy with a stroke of popularity.

Thus every Secretary of State is duly warned that whenever his master takes the road heavenward, he must become lost again in the common herd of the Sacred College. He feels, therefore, that he ought to make the best possible use of his time.

He has, moreover, the comfortable assurance that after his disgrace, he will not be called upon for any account of his past deeds; for the least of the Cardinals is as inviolable as the twelve Apostles. Surely, then, he would be a fool to refuse anything while he has the power to take it.

This is the place to sketch, in a few pages, the portraits of the two men,—one of whom possesses, and the other exercises, the dictatorship over three millions of unfortunate beings.

CHAPTER X.

PIUS IX.

OLD age, majesty, and misfortune have a claim to the respect of all right-minded persons: fear not that I shall be wanting in such respect.

But truth has also its claims: it also is old, it is majestic, it is holy, and it is sometimes cruelly ill-treated by men.

I shall not forget that the Pope is sixty-seven years of age, that he wears a crown officially venerated by a hundred and thirty-nine millions of Catholics, that his private life has ever been exemplary, that he observes the most noble disinterestedness upon a throne where selfishness has long held sway, that he spontaneously commenced his reign by conferring benefits, that his first acts held out the fairest hopes to Italy and to Europe, that he has suffered the lingering torture of exile, that he exercises a precarious and dependent royalty under the protection of two foreign armies, and that he lives under the control of a Cardinal. But those who have fallen victims to the efforts made to replace him on his throne, those whom the Austrians have, at his request, shot and sabred, in order to re-establish his authority, and even those who toil in the plague-stricken plains of the Roman Campagna to fill his treasury, are far more to be pitied than he is.

Giovanni-Maria, dei Conti Mastai Ferretti, born the 13th

May, 1792, and elected Pope the 16th June, 1846, under the name of Pius IX., is a man who looks more than his actual age; he is short, obese, somewhat pallid, and in precarious health. His benevolent and sleepy countenance breathes good-nature and lassitude, but has nothing of an imposing character. Gregory XVI., though ugly and pimply, is said to have had a grand air.

Pius IX. plays his part in the gorgeous shows of the Roman Catholic Church indifferently well. The faithful who have come from afar to see him perform Mass, are a little surprised to see him take a pinch of snuff in the midst of the azure-tinted clouds of incense. In his hours of leisure he plays at billiards for exercise, by order of his physicians.

He believes in God. He is not only a good Christian, but a devotee. In his enthusiasm for the Virgin Mary, he has invented a useless dogma, and disfigured the Piazza di Spagna by a monument of bad taste. His morals are pure, as they always have been, even when he was a young priest: such instances are common enough among our clergy, but rare, not to say miraculous, beyond the Alps.

He has nephews, who, wonderful to relate, are neither rich nor powerful, nor even princes. And yet there is no law which prevents him from spoiling his subjects for the benefit of his family. Gregory XIII. gave his nephew Ludovisi £160,000 of good paper, worth so much cash. The Borghese family bought at one stroke ninety-five farms with the money of Paul V. A commission which met in 1640, under the presidence of the Reverend Father Vitelleschi, General of the Jesuits, decided, in order to put an end to such abuses, that the Popes should confine themselves to entailing property to the amount of £16,000 a year upon their favourite nephew and his family (with the right of creating a second heir to the same privileges), and that the portion of each of their nieces should not exceed £36,000.

I am aware that nepotism fell into desuetude at the commencement of the eighteenth century; but there was nothing to prevent Pius IX. from bringing it into fashion again, after the example of Pius VI., if he chose; but he does not choose to do so. His relations are of the second order of nobility, and are not rich: he has done nothing to alter their position. His nephew, Count Mastai Ferretti, was recently married; and the Pope's wedding present consisted of a few diamonds, worth about £8000. Nor did this modest gift cost the nation one baioccho. The diamonds came from the Sovereign of Turkey. Some ten years ago the Sultan of Constantinople, the Commander of the Faithful, presented the commander of the unfaithful with a saddle embroidered with precious stones. The travellers in the restoring line, who used to flock to Gaeta and Portici, carried off a great number of them in their bags; what they left are in the casket of the young Countess Ferretti.

The character of this respectable old man, is made up of devotion, simplicity, vanity, weakness, and obstinacy, with an occasional touch of rancour. He blesses with unction, and pardons with difficulty; he is a good priest, and an insufficient king.

His intellect, which has raised such great hopes, and caused such cruel disappointment, is of a very ordinary capacity. I can hardly think he is infallible in temporal matters. His education is that of the average of cardinals in general. He talks French pretty well.

The Romans formed an exaggerated opinion of him at his accession, and have done so ever since. In 1847, when he honestly manifested a desire to do good, they called him a great man, whereas in point of fact he was simply a worthy man who wished to act better than his predecessors had done, and thereby to win some applause from Europe. In 1859, he passes for a violent re-actionist, because events have discouraged his good intentions: and above all, because Cardinal Antonelli, who masters him by fear, violently draws him backwards. I consider him as meriting neither past admiration nor present hatred. I pity him for having loosened the rein upon his people, without possessing the firmness requisite to restrain them seasonably. I pity still more that infirmity of character which now allows more evil to be done in his name than he has ever himself done good.

The failure of all his enterprises, and three or four accidents which happened in his presence, have given rise to the popular belief that the Vicar of Jesus Christ is what the Italians call *jettatore*—in other words, that he has the *evil eye*. When he drives along the Corso, the old women fall down on their knees, but they snap their fingers at him beneath their cloaks.

The members of the Italian secret societies impute to him—though for other reasons—all the evils which afflict their country. It is evident that the Italian question would be greatly simplified, if there were no Pope at Rome; but the hatred of the Mazzinists against Pius IX. is to be condemned in all its personal aspects. They would kill him to a certainty, if our troops were not there to defend him. This murder would be as unjust as that of Louis XVI., and as useless. The guillotine would deprive a good old man of his life, but it would not put an end to the bad principle of sacerdotal monarchy.

I did not seek an audience of Pius IX.; I neither kissed his hand nor his slipper; the only mark of attention I received from him was a few lines of insult in the *Giornale di*

Roma. Still, I never can hear him accused without defending him.

Let my readers for a moment put themselves in the place of this too illustrious and too unfortunate old man. After having been for nearly two years the favourite of public opinion, and the *lion* of Europe, he found himself obliged to quit the Quirinal palace at a moment's notice. At Gaeta and Portici he tasted those lingering hours which sour the spirit of the exile. A grand and time-honoured principle, of which the legitimacy is not doubtful to him, was violated in his person. His advisers unanimously said to him: "It is your own fault. You have endangered the monarchy by your ideas of progress. The immobility of governments is the *sine quâ non* of the stability of thrones. You will not doubt this, if you read again the history of your predecessors." He had had time to become converted to this belief, when the armies of the Catholic powers once more opened for him the road to Rome. Overjoyed at seeing the principle saved, he vowed to himself never again to compromise it, but to reign without progress, according to papal tradition. But these very foreign powers who had saved his crown, were the first to impose on him the condition of advancing! What was to be done? He was equally afraid to promise everything, and to refuse everything. After a long hesitation, he promised in spite of himself; then he absolved himself, for the sake of the future, from the engagements he had made for the sake of the present.

Now he is out of humour with his people, with the French, and with himself. He knows the nation is suffering, but he allows himself to be persuaded that the misfortunes of the nation are indispensable to the safety of the Church. Those about him take care that the reproaches of his conscience shall be stifled by the recollections of 1848 and the dread of a new revolution. He stops his eyes and his ears, and prepares to die calmly between his furious subjects on one hand, and his dissatisfied protectors on the other. Any man wanting in energy, placed as he is, would behave exactly in the same manner. The fault is not his, it is that of weakness and old-age.

But I do not undertake to obtain the acquittal of his Minister of State, Cardinal Antonelli

CHAPTER XI.

ANTONELLI.

He was born in a den of thieves. His native place, Sonnino, is more celebrated in the history of crime than all Arcadia in the annals of virtue. This nest of vultures was hidden in the southern mountains, towards the Neapolitan frontier. Roads, impracticable to mounted dragoons, winding through brakes and thickets; forests, impenetrable to the stranger; deep ravines and gloomy caverns,—all combined to form a most desirable landscape, for the convenience of crime. The houses of Sonnino, old, ill-built, flung pell-mell one upon the other, and almost uninhabitable by human beings, were, in point of fact, little else than depots of pillage and magazines of rapine. The population, alert and vigorous, had for many centuries practised armed robbery and depredation, and gained its livelihood at the point of the carbine. New-born infants inhaled contempt of the law with the mountain air, and drew in the love of others' goods with their mothers' milk. Almost as soon as they could walk, they assumed the *cioccie*, or mocassins of untanned leather, with which they learned to run fearlessly along the edge of the giddiest mountain precipices. When they had acquired the art of pursuing and escaping, of taking without being taken, the knowledge of the value of the different coins, the arithmetic of the distribution of booty, and the principles of the rights of nations as they are practised among the Apaches or the Comanches, their education was deemed complete. They required no teaching to learn how to apply the spoil, and to satisfy their passions in the hour of victory.

In the year of grace 1806, this sensual, brutal, impious, superstitious, ignorant, and cunning race endowed Italy with a little mountaineer, known as Giacomo Antonelli.

Hawks do not hatch doves. This is an axiom in natural history which has no need of demonstration. Had Giacomo Antonelli been gifted at his birth with the simple virtues of an Arcadian shepherd, his village would have instantly disowned him. But the influence of certain events modified his conduct, although they failed to modify his nature. His infancy and his childhood were subjected to two opposing influences. If he received his earliest lessons from successful brigandage, his next teachers were the gendarmerie. When he was hardly four years old, the discharge of a high moral lesson shook his ears : it was the French troops who were shooting brigands in the outskirts of Sonnino. After the return of Pius VII. he witnessed the decapitation of a few neighbouring relatives who had often dandled him on their knees. Under Leo XII. it was still worse. Those wholesome correctives, the wooden horse and the supple-jack, were permanently established in the village square. About once a fortnight the authorities rased the house of some brigand, after sending his family to the galleys, and paying a reward to the informer who had denounced him. St. Peter's Gate, which adjoins the house of the Antonellis, was ornamented with a garland of human heads, which eloquent relics grinned dogmatically enough in their iron cages. If the stage be a school of life, surely such a stage as this is a rare teacher. Young Giacomo was enabled to reflect upon the inconveniences of brigandage, even before he had tasted its sweets. About him some men of progress had already engaged in industrial pursuits of a less hazardous nature than robbery. His own father, who, it was whispered, had in him the stuff of a Gasparone or a Passatore, instead of exposing himself upon the highways, took to keeping bullocks, he then became an Intendant, and subsequently was made a Municipal Receiver; by which occupations he acquired more money at considerably less risk.

The young Antonelli hesitated for some time as to the choice of a calling. His natural vocation was that of the inhabitants of Sonnino in general, to live in plenty, to enjoy every sort of pleasure, to make himself at home everywhere, to be dependent upon nobody, to rule others, and to frighten them, if necessary, but, above all, to violate the laws with impunity. With the view of attaining so lofty an end without exposing his life, for which he ever had a most particular regard, he entered the great seminary of Rome.

In our land of scepticism, a young man enters the seminary with the hope of being ordained a priest: Antonelli entered it with the opposite intention. But in the capital of the Catholic Church, young Levites of ordinary intelligence become magistrates, prefects, councillors of state, and ministers, while the "dry fruit* is thought good enough for making priests."

Antonelli so distinguished himself, that (with Heaven's help) he escaped the sacrament of Ordination. He has never said mass: he has never confessed a penitent; I won't swear he has even confessed himself. He gained what was of more value than all the Christian virtues—the friendship of Gregory XVI. He became a prelate, a magistrate, a prefect,

* An expression in use among collegians in France, to describe those students who are unable to pass their examinations; tantamount to our English *plucked*.

Secretary General of the Interior, and Minister of Finance. No one can say he has not chosen the right path. A finance minister, if he knows anything of his business, can lay by more money in six months than all the brigands of Sonnino in twenty years.

Under Gregory XVI. he had been a reactionist, to please his sovereign. On the accession of Pius IX., for the same reason, he professed liberal ideas. A red hat and a ministerial portfolio were the recompense of his new convictions, and proved to the inhabitants of Sonnino that liberalism itself is more lucrative than brigandage. What a practical lesson for those mountaineers! One of themselves clothed in purple and fine linen, actually riding in his gilt coach, passed the barracks, and their old friends the dragoons presenting arms, instead of firing long shots at him!

He obtained the same influence over the new Pope that he had over the old one, thus proving that people may be got hold of without stopping them on the highway. Pius IX., who had no secrets from him, confided to him his wish to correct abuses, without concealing his fear of succeeding too well. He served the Holy Father, even in his irresolutions. As President of the Supreme Council of State, he proposed reforms, and as Minister he postponed their adoption. Nobody was more active than he, whether in settling or in violating the constitution of 1848. He sent Durando to fight the Austrians, and disavowed him after the battle.

He quitted the ministry as soon as he found there were dangers to be encountered, but assisted the Pope in his secret opposition to his ministers. The murder of Count Rossi gave him serious cause for reflection. A man don't take the trouble to be born at Sonnino, in order to let himself be assassinated: quite the contrary. He placed the Pope—and himself—in safety, and then went to Gaeta to play the part of Secretary of State *in partibus.*

From this exile dates his omnipotence over the will of the Holy Father, his reinstatement in the esteem of the Austrians, and the consistency in his whole conduct. Since then no more contradictions in his political life. They who formally accused him of hesitating between the welfare of the nation and his own personal interest are reduced to silence. He wishes to restore the absolute power of the Pope, in order that he may dispose of it at his ease. He prevents all reconciliation between Pius IX. and his subjects; he summons the cannon of Catholicism to effect the conquest of Rome. He ill-uses the French, who are willing to die for him; he turns a deaf ear to the liberal counsels of Napoleon III.; he designedly prolongs the exile of his master; he draws up the promises of the *Motu Proprio*, while devising means to elude them. At length, he returns to Rome, and for ten years continues to reign over a timid old man and an enslaved people, opposing a passive resistance to all the counsels of diplomacy and all the demands of Europe. Clinging tenaciously to power, reckless as to the future, misusing present opportunities, and day by day increasing his fortune—after the manner of Sonnino.

In this year of grace 1859, he is fifty-three years of age. He presents the appearance of a well-preserved man. His frame is slight and robust, and his constitution is that of a mountaineer. The breadth of his forehead, the brilliancy of his eyes, his beak-like nose, and all the upper part of his face inspire a certain awe. His countenance, of almost Moorish hue, is at times lit up by flashes of intellect. But his heavy jaw, his long fang-like teeth, and his thick lips express the grossest appetites. He gives you the idea of a minister grafted on a savage. When he assists the Pope in the ceremonies of the Holy Week he is magnificently disdainful and impertinent. He turns from time to time in the direction of the diplomatic tribune, and looks without a smile at the poor ambassadors, whom he cajoles from morning to night. You admire the actor who bullies his public. But when at an evening party he engages in close conversation with a handsome woman, the play of his countenance shows the direction of his thoughts, and those of the imaginative observer are imperceptibly carried to a roadside in a lonely forest, in which the principal objects are prostrate postilions, an overturned carriage, trembling females, and a select party of the inhabitants of Sonnino!

He lives in the Vatican, immediately over the Pope. The Romans ask punningly which is the uppermost, the Pope or Antonelli?

All classes of society hate him equally. Concini himself was not more cordially detested. He is the only living man concerning whom an entire people is agreed.

A Roman prince furnished me with some information respecting the relative fortunes of the nobility. When he gave me the list he said, " You will remark the names of two individuals, the amount of whose property is described as unlimited. They are Torlonia and Antonelli. They have both made large fortunes in a few years,—the first by speculation, the second by power."

The Cardinals Altieri and Antonelli were one day disputing upon some point in the Pope's presence. They flatly contradicted one another; and the Pope inclined to the opinion of his Minister. " Since your Holiness," said the noble Altieri, " accords belief to a *ciociari* * rather than to a Roman prince, I have nothing to do but to withdraw."

* A man who has worn *ciocie.*

The Apostles themselves appear to entertain no very amicable feelings towards the Secretary of State. The last time the Pope made a solemn entry into his capital (I think it was after his journey to Bologna), the Porta del Popolo and the Corso were according to custom hung with draperies, behind which the old statues of St. Peter and St. Paul were completely hidden. Accordingly the people were entertained by finding the following dialogue appended to the corner of the street:—

Peter to Paul. "It seems to me, old fellow, that we are somewhat forsaken here."

Paul to Peter. "What would you have? We are no longer anything. There is but James in the world now."

I am aware that hatred proves nothing—even the hatred of Apostles. The French nation, which claims to be thought just, insulted the funeral procession of Louis XIV. It also occasionally detested Henri IV. for his economy, and Napoleon for his victories. No statesman should be judged upon the testimony of his enemies. The only evidence we should admit either for or against him, is his public acts. The only witnesses to which any weight should be attributed are the greatness and the prosperity of the country he governs.

Such an inquiry would, I fear, be ruinous to Antonelli. The nation reproaches him with all the evils it has suffered for the last ten years. The public wretchedness and ignorance, the decline of the arts, the entire suppression of liberty, the ever-present curse of foreign occupation,—all fall upon his head, because he alone is responsible for everything.

It may be alleged that he has at least served the reactionary party. I much doubt it. What internal factions has he suppressed? Secret societies have swarmed in Rome during his reign. What remonstrances from without has he silenced? Europe continues to complain unanimously, and day by day lifts up its voice a tone or two higher. He has failed to reconcile one single party or one single power to the Holy father. During his ten years' dictatorship, he has neither gained the esteem of one foreigner nor the confidence of one Roman. All he has gained is time. His pretended capacity is but slyness. To the trickery of the present he adds the cunning of the red Indian; but he has not that largeness of view without which it is impossible to establish firmly the slavery of the people. No one possesses in a greater degree than he the art of dragging on an affair, and manœuvring with and tiring out diplomatists; but it is not by pleasantries of this sort that a tottering tyranny can be propped up. Although he employs every subterfuge known to dishonest policy, I am not quite sure that he has even the craft of a politician.

The attainment of his own end does not in fact require it. For after all, what is his end? In what hope, with what aim, did he come down from the mountains of Sonnino?

Do you really believe he thought of becoming the benefactor of the nation?—or the saviour of the Papacy?—or the Don Quixote of the Church? Not such a fool! He thought, first, of himself; secondly, of his family.

His family is flourishing. His four brothers, Filippo, Luigi, Gregorio, and—save the mark!—Angelo, all wore the *cioccie* in their younger days; they now, one and all, wear the count's coronet. One is governor of the bank, a capital post, and since poor Campana's condemnation he has got the Monte di Pietà. Another is Conservator of Rome, under a Senator especially selected for his incapacity. Another follows openly the trape of a monopolist, with immense facilities for either preventing or authorizing exportation, according as his own warehouses happen to be full or empty. The youngest is the commercial traveller, the diplomatist, the messenger of the family, *Angelus Domini*. A cousin of the family, Count Dandini, reigns over the police. This little group is perpetually at work adding to a fortune which is invisible, impalpable, and incalculable. The house of Antonelli is not pitied at Sonnino.

As for the Secretary of State, all who know him intimately, both men and women, agree that he leads a pleasant life. If it were not for the bore of making head against the diplomatists, and giving audience every morning, he would be the happiest of mountaineers. His tastes are simple; a scarlet silk robe, unlimited power, an enormous fortune, a European reputation, and all the pleasures within man's reach—this trifle satisfies the simple tastes of the Cardinal Minister. Add, by the bye, a splendid collection of minerals, perfectly classified which he is constantly enriching with the passion of an amateur and the tenderness of a father.

I was saying just now that he has always escaped the sacrament of Holy Orders. He is Cardinal Deacon. The good souls who will have it that all goes well at Rome, dwell with fervour on the advantage he possesses in not being a priest. If he is accused of possessing inordinate wealth, these indulgent Christians reply, that he is not a priest! If you charge him with having read Machiavelli to good purpose; admitted—what then?—he is no priest! If the tongue of scandal is over-free with his private life; still the ready reply, that he is not a priest! If Deacons are thus privileged, what latitude may we not claim who have not even assumed the tonsure?

This highly-blest mortal has one weakness—truly a very natural one. He fears death. A certain fair lady, who had been honoured by his Eminence's particular attentions, thus illustrated the fact. "Upon meeting me at our rendezvous, he seized me like a madman, and with trembling eagerness examined my pockets. It was only when he had assured himself that I had no concealed weapon about me that he seemed to remember our friendship."

One man alone has dared to threaten a life so precious to itself, and he was an idiot. Instigated by some of the secret societies, this poor crazed wretch concealed himself beneath the staircase of the Vatican, and awaited the coming of the Cardinal. When the intended victim appeared, the idiot with much difficulty drew from beneath his waistcoat—a table-fork! Antonelli saw the terrible weapon, and bounded backwards with a spring which an Alpine chamois-hunter might have envied. The miserable assassin was instantly seized, bound, and delivered over to justice. The Roman tribunals, so often lenient towards the really guilty, had no mercy for this real innocent. He was beheaded. The Cardinal, full of pity, fell—officially—at the Pope's feet, and asked for a pardon which he well knew would be refused. He pays the widow a pension : is not this the act of a clever man ?

Since the day when that formidable fork glittered before his eyes, he has taken excessive precautions. His horses are broken to gallop furiously through the streets, at considerable public risk. Occasionally, his carriage knocks down and runs over a little boy or girl. With characteristic magnanimity, he sends the parents fifty crowns.

Antonelli has been compared to Mazarin. They have, in common, the fear of death, inordinate love of money, a strong family feeling, utter indifference to the people's welfare, contempt for mankind, and some other accidental points of resemblance. They were born in the same mountains, or nearly so. One obtained the influence over a woman's heart which the other possesses over the mind of an old man.

Both governed unscrupulously, and both have merited and obtained the hatred of their contemporaries. They have talked French comically, without being insensible to any of the delicate niceties of the language.

Still there would be manifest injustice in placing them in the same rank. The selfish Mazarin dictated to Europe the treaties of Westphalia, and the Peace of the Pyrenees: he founded by diplomacy the greatness of Louis XIV., and managed the affairs of the French monarchy, without in any way neglecting his own.

Antonelli has made his fortnne at the expense of the nation, the Pope, and the Church. Mazarin may be compared to a skilful but rascally tailor, who dresses his customers well, while he contrives to cabbage sundry yards of their cloth; Antonelli, to those Jews of the Middle Ages, who demolished the Coliseum for the sake of the old iron in the walls.

CHAPTER XII.

PRIESTLY GOVERNMENT.

If the Pope were merely the head of the Roman Catholic Church; if, limiting his action to the interior of temples, he would renounce the sway over temporal matters about which he knows nothing, his countrymen of Rome, Ancona, and Bologna might govern themselves as people do in London or in Paris. The administration would be lay, the laws would be lay, the nation would provide for its own wants with its own revenues, as is the custom in all civilized countries.

As for the general expenses of the Roman Catholic worship, which in point of fact no more *specially* concern the Romans than they do the Champenois, a voluntary contribution made by one hundred and thirty-nine millions of men would amply provide for them. If each individual among the faithful were to give a halfpenny *per annum*, the head of the Church would have something like £300,000 to spend upon his wax tapers and his incense, his choristers and his sacristans, and the repairs of the basilica of St. Peter's. No Roman Catholic would think of refusing his quota, because the Holy Father, entirely separated from worldly interests, would not be in a position to offend anybody. This small tax would, therefore, restore independence to the Romans without diminishing the independence of the Pope.

Unfortunately the Pope is a king. In this capacity he

must have a Court, or something approaching to it. He selects his courtiers among men of his own faith, his own opinions, and his own profession: nothing can be more reasonable. These courtiers, in their turn, dispose of the different offices of state, spiritual or temporal, just as it may happen. Nor can the Sovereign object to this pretension as being ridiculous. Moreover he naturally hopes to be more faithfully served by priests than laymen; while he feels that the salaries attached to the best-paid places are necessary to the splendour of his Court.

Thence it follows that to preach the secularization of the government to the Pope, is to preach to the winds. Here you have a man who would not be a layman, who pities laymen simply because they are laymen, regarding them as a caste inferior to his own; who has received an anti-lay education; who thinks differently to laymen on all important points; and you expect this man will share his power with laymen, in an empire where he is absolute master of all and everything! You require him to surround himself with laymen, to summon them to his councils, and to confide to them the execution of his behests!

Supposing, however, that for some reason or other he fears you, and wishes to humour you a little, see what he will do. He will seek in the outer offices of his ministers some lay secretary, or assistant, or clerk, a man without character or talent; he will employ him, and take care that his incapacity shall be universally known and admitted. After which, he will say to you sadly, "I have done what I could." But if he were to speak the honest truth, he would at once say, "If you wish to secularize anything, begin by putting laymen in *my* place."

It is not in 1859 that the Pope will venture to speak so haughtily. Intimidated by the protection of France, deafened by the unanimous complaints of his subjects, obliged to reckon with public opinion, he declares that he has secularized everything. "Count my functionaries," he says; "I have 14,576 laymen in my service. You have been told that ecclesiastics monopolize the public service. Show me these ecclesiastics! The Count de Rayneval looked for them, and could find but ninety-eight; and even of those, the greater part were not in priests' orders! Be assured we have long since broken with the clerical *régime*. I myself decreed the admissibility of laymen to all offices but one. In order to show my sincerity, for some time I had lay ministers! I entrusted the finances to a mere accountant, the department of justice to an obscure little advocate, and that of war to a man of business who had been intendant to several Cardinals. I admit that for the moment we have no laymen in the Ministry; but my subjects may console themselves by reflecting that the law does not prevent me from appointing them.

"In the provinces, out of eighteen prefects, I appointed three laymen. If I afterwards substituted prelates for those three, it was because the people loudly called for the change. Is it my fault if the people respect nothing but the ecclesiastical garb?"

This style of defence may deceive some good easy folk; but I think if I were Pope, or Secretary of State, or even a simple supporter of the Pontifical administration, I should prefer telling the plain truth. That truth is strictly logical, it is in conformity with the principle of the Government; it emanates from the Constitution. Things are exactly what they ought to be, if not for the welfare of the people, at least for the greatness, security, and satisfaction of its temporal head.

The truth then is that all the ministers, all the prefects, all the ambassadors, all the court dignitaries, and all the judges of the superior tribunals, are ecclesiastics; that the Secretary of the *Brevi* and the *Memoriali*, the Presidents and Vice-Presidents of the Council of State and the Council of Finances, the Director-General of the Police, the Director of Public Health and Prisons, the Director of the Archives, the Attorney-General of the Fisc, the President and the Secretary of the *Cadastro*, the Agricultural President and Commission, are *all ecclesiastics*. The public education is in the hands of ecclesiastics, under the direction of thirteen Cardinals. All the charitable establishments, all the funds applicable to the relief of the poor, are the patrimony of ecclesiastical directors. Congregations of Cardinals decide causes in their leisure hours, and the Bishops of the kingdom are so many living tribunals.

Why seek to conceal from Europe so natural an order of things?

Let Europe rather be told what it did when it re-established a priest on the throne of Rome.

All the offices which confer power or profit belong first to the Pope, then to the Secretary of State, then to the Cardinals, and lastly to the Prelates. Everybody takes his share according to the hierarchical order; and when all are satisfied, the crumbs of power are thrown to the nation at large; in other words, the 14,596 places which no ecclesiastic chooses to take, particularly the distinguished office of *Guardia Campestre*, a sort of rural police. Nobody need wonder at such a distribution of places. In the government of Rome, the Pope is everything, the Secretary of State is almost everything, the Cardinals are something, and the priests on the road to become something. The *lay nation*, which marries and gives in marriage, and peoples the State, is nothing—never will be anything.

The word *prelate* has fallen from my pen; I will pause

a moment to explain its precise meaning. Among us it is a title sufficiently respected: at Rome it is far less so. We have no prelates but our Archbishops and Bishops. When we see one of these venerable men driving slowly out of his palace in an old-fashioned carriage drawn by a single pair of horses, we know, without being told it, that he has spent three-fourths of his existence in the exercise of the most meritorious works. He said Mass in some small village before he was made the cure of a canton. He has preached, confessed, distributed alms to the poor, borne the viaticum to the sick, committed the dead to their last narrow home.

The Roman prelate is often a great hulking fellow who has just left college, with the tonsure for his only sacrament. He is a Doctor of something or other, he owns some property, more or less, and he enters the Church as an amateur, to see if he can make something out of it. The Pope gives him leave to style himself *Monsignore*, instead of *Signore*, and to wear violet-coloured stockings. Clad in these he starts on his road, hoping it may lead him to a Cardinal's hat. He passes through the courts of law, or the administration, or the domestic service of the Vatican, as the case may be. All these paths lead in the right direction, provided the traveller pursuing them has zeal, and professes a pious scorn for liberal ideas. The ecclesiastical calling is by no means indispensable, but nothing can be achieved without a good stock of retrograde ideas. The prelate who should take the Emperor's letter to M. Edgar Ney seriously, would be, in vulgar parlance, done for; the only course open to him would be—to marry. At Paris, a man disappointed in ambition takes prussic acid; at Rome, he takes a wife.

Sometimes the prelate is a cadet of a noble house, one in which the right to a red hat is traditional. Knowing this he feels that the moment he puts on his violet stockings, he may order his scarlet ones. In the meanwhile he takes his degrees, and profits by the occasion to sow his wild oats. The Cardinals shut their eyes to his conduct, so he does but profess wholesome ideas. Do what you please, child of princes, so your heart be but clerical!

Finally, it is not uncommon to find among the prelates some soldiers of fortune, adventurers of the Church, who have been attracted from their native land by the ambition of ecclesiastical greatness. This corps of volunteers receives contingents from the whole Catholic world. These gentlemen furnish some strange examples to the Roman people; and I know more than one of them to whom mothers of families would on no account confide the education of their children. It has happened to me to have described in a novel* a prelate who richly deserved a thrashing; the good folks of Rome have named to me three or four whom they fancied they recognized in the portrait. But it has never yet been known that any prelate, however vicious, has given utterance to liberal ideas. A single word from a Roman prelate's lips in behalf of the nation would ruin him.

The Count de Rayneval has laboured hard to prove that prelates, who have not received the sacrament of Ordination, form part of the lay element. At this rate, a province should deem itself fortunate, and think it has escaped priestly government, if its prefect is simply tonsured. I cannot for the life of me see in what tonsured prelates are more laymen than they are priests. I admit that they neither follow the calling nor possess the virtues of the priesthood; but I maintain that they have the ideas, the interests, the passions of the ecclesiastical caste. They aim at the Cardinal's hat, when their ambition does not soar to the tiara. Singular laymen, truly, and well fitted to inspire confidence in a lay

* '*Tolla.*' 1 vol. 12mo.

people! 'Twere better they should become Cardinals; for then they would no longer have their fortunes to make, and they would not be called upon to signalize their zeal against the nation.

For that is, unhappily, the state at which things have arrived. This same ecclesiastical caste, so strongly united by the bonds of a learned hierarchy, reigns as over a conquered country. It regards the middle class,—in other words, the intelligent and laborious part of the nation,—as an irreconcilable foe. The prefects are ordered, not to govern the provinces, but to keep them in order. The police is kept, not to protect the citizens, but to watch them. The tribunals have other interests to defend than those of justice. The diplomatic body does not represent a country, but a coterie. The educating body has the mission not to teach, but to prevent the spread of instruction. The taxes are not a national assessment, but an official foray for the profit of certain ecclesiastics. Examine all the departments of the public administration: you will everywhere find the clerical element at war with the nation, and of course everywhere victorious.

In this state of things it is idle to say to the Pope, "Fill your principal offices with laymen." You might as well say to Austria, "Place your fortresses under the guard of the Piedmontese." The Roman administration is what it must be. It will remain what it is as long as there is a Pope on the throne.

Besides, although the lay population still complains of being systematically excluded from power, matters have reached such a point, that an honest man of the middle class would think himself dishonoured by accepting a high post. It would be said that he had deserted the nation to serve the enemy.

CHAPTER XIII.

POLITICAL SEVERITY.

It is admitted that the Popes have always been remarkable for a senile indulgence and goodness. I do not pretend to deny the assertions of M. de Brosses and M. de Tournon that this government is at once the mildest, the worst, and the most absolute in Europe.

And yet Sixtus V., a great Pope, was a still greater executioner. That man of God delivered over to the gallows a Pepoli of Bologna, who had bestowed upon him a kick instead of a piece of bread when he was a mendicant friar.

And yet Gregory XVI., in our own times, granted a dispensation of age to a minor for the sake of having him legally executed.

And yet the punishment of the wooden horse was revived four years ago by the mild Cardinal Antonelli.

And yet the Pontifical State is the only one in Europe in which the barbarous practice of placing a price upon a man's head is still in use.

Never mind. Since, after all, the Pontifical State is that in which the most daring crimes and the most open assassinations have the greatest chance of being committed with perfect impunity, I will admit, with M. de Brosses and M. de Tournon, that it is the mildest in Europe.

I am about to examine with you the application of this mildness to political matters.

Nine years ago Pius IX. re-entered his capital, as the father of a family his house, after having the door broken open. It is not likely that either the Holy Father, or the companions of his exile, were animated by very lively feelings of gratitude towards the chiefs of the revolution which had driven them away. A priest never quite forgets that he was once a man.

This is why two hundred and eighty-three individuals* were excluded from the general amnesty recommended by France and promised by the Pope. It is unfortunate for these two hundred and eighty-three that the Gospel is old, and forgiveness of injuries out of date. Perhaps you will remind me that St. Peter cut off one of the ears of Malchus.

By the clemency of the Pope, fifty-nine of these exiles were pardoned, during a period of nine years, if men can be said to be pardoned who are recalled provisionally, some for a year, others for half a year, or who are brought home only to be placed under the surveillance of the police. A man who is forbidden to exercise the calling to which he was bred, and whose sole privilege is that of dying of starvation in his native land, is likely rather to regret his exile sometimes.

I was introduced to one of the fifty-nine privileged partakers of the pontifical clemency. He is an advocate; at least he was until the day when he obtained his pardon. He related to me the history of the tolerably inoffensive part he had played in 1848; the hopes he had founded on the amnesty; his despair when he found himself excluded from it; some particulars of his life in exile, such, for instance, as his

* 'The Victories of the Church,' by the Priest Margotti. 1857.

having had recourse to giving lessons in Italian, like the illustrious Manin, and so many others.

"I could have lived happily enough," he said, "but one day the home-sickness laid my heart low; I felt that I must see Italy, or die. My family took the necessary steps, and it fortunately happened that we knew some one who had interest with a Cardinal. The police dictated the conditions of my return, and I accepted them without knowing what they were. If they had told me I could not return without cutting off my right arm, I would have cut it off. The Pope signed my pardon, and then published my name in the newspapers, so that none might be ignorant of his clemency. But I am interdicted from resuming my practice at the Bar, and a man can hardly gain a livelihood by teaching Italian in a country where everybody speaks it."

As he concluded, the neighbouring church-bells began to sound the *Ave Maria.* He turned pale, seized his hat, and rushed out of my room, exclaiming, "I knew not it was so late! Should the police arrive at my house before I can reach it, I am a lost man!"

His friends explained to me the cause of his sudden alarm: the poor man is subject to the police regulation termed the *Precetto.*

He must always return to his abode at sunset, and he is then shut in till the next morning. The police may force their way in at any time during the night, for the purpose of ascertaining that he is there. He cannot leave the city under any pretence whatever, even in broad day. The slightest infraction of these rules exposes him to imprisonment, or to a new exile.

The Pontifical States are full of men subject to the *Precetto:* some are criminals who are watched in their homes, for want of prison accommodation; others are *suspected per-*

sons. The number of these unfortunate beings is not given in the statistical tables, but I know, from an official source, that in Viterbo, a town of fourteen thousand souls, there are no less than two hundred.

The want of prison accommodation explains many things, and, among others, the freedom of speech which exists throughout the country. If the Government took a fancy to arrest everybody who hates it openly, there would be neither gendarmes nor gaolers enough; above all, there would be an insufficiency of those houses of peace, of which it has been said, that "their potection and salubrity prolong the life of their inmates."*

The citizens, then, are allowed to speak freely, provided always they do not gesticulate too violently. But we may be sure no word is ever lost in a State watched by priests. The Government keeps an accurate list of those who wish it ill. It revenges itself when it can, but it never runs after vengeance. It watches its occasion; it can afford to be patient, because it thinks itself eternal.

If the bold speaker chance to hold a modest government appointment, a purging commission quietly cashiers him, and turns him delicately out into the street.

Should he be a person of independent fortune, they wait till he wants something, as, for instance, a passport. One of my good friends in Rome has been for the last nine years trying to get leave to travel. He is rich and energetic. The business he follows is one eminently beneficial to the State. A journey to foreign countries would complete his knowledge, and advance his interests. For the last nine years he has been applying for an interview with the head of the pass-

* 'Proemio della Statistica,' pubblicata nel 1857, dall' Eminentissimo Cardinale Milesi.

port office, and has never yet received an answer to his application.

Others, who have applied for permission to travel in Piedmont, have received for answer, "Go, but return no more." They have not been exiled; there is no need of exercising unnecessary rigour; but on receiving their passports, they have been compelled to sign an act of voluntary exile. The Greeks said, "Not every one who will goes to Corinth." The Romans have substituted Turin for Corinth.

Another of my friends, the Count X., has been, for years, carrying on a lawsuit before the infallible tribunal of the SACRA ROTA. His cause could not have been a bad one, seeing that he lost and gained it some seven or eight times before the same judges. It assumed a deplorably bad complexion from the day the Count became my friend.

When once the discontented proceed from words to actions you may indeed pity them.

A person charged with a political offence summoned before the SACRA CONSULTA (for everything is holy and sacred, even justice and injustice), must be defended by an advocate, not chosen by himself, against witnesses whose very names are unknown to him.

In the capital (and under the eyes of the French army) the extreme penalty of the law is rarely carried out. The government is satisfied with quietly suppressing people, by shutting them up in a fortress for life. The state prisons are of two sorts, healthy and unhealthy. In the establishment coming within the second category, perpetual seclusion is certain not to be of very long duration.

The fortress of Pagliano is one of the most wholesome. When I walked through it there were two hundred and fifty prisoners, all political. The people of the country told me that in 1856 these unfortunate men had made an attempt at escape. Five or six had been shot on the roof like so many sparrows. The remainder, according to the common law, would be liable to the galleys for eight years; but an old ordinance of Cardinal Lante was revived, by which, God willing, some of them may be guillotined.

It is, however, beyond the Apennines that the paternal character of the Government is chiefly displayed. The French are not there, and the Pope's reactionary police duty is performed by the Austrian army. The law there is martial law. The prisoner is without counsel; his judges are Austrian officers, his executioners Austrian soldiers. A man may be beaten or shot because some gentleman in uniform happens to be in a bad temper. A youth sends up a Bengal light,—the galleys for twenty years. A woman prevents a smoker from lighting his cigar,—twenty lashes. In seven years Ancona has witnessed sixty capital executions, and Bologna a hundred and eighty. Blood flows, and the Pope washes his hands of it. He did not sign the warrants. Every now and then the Austrians bring him a man they have shot, just as a gamekeeper brings his master a fox he has killed in the preserves.

Perhaps I shall be told that this government of priests is not responsible for the crimes committed in its service.

We French have also experienced the scourge of a foreign occupation. For some years soldiers who spoke not our language were encamped in our departments. The king who had been forced upon us was neither a great man nor a man of energy, nor even a very good man; and he had left a portion of his dignity in the enemy's baggage-waggons. But certain it is that, in 1817, Louis XVIII. would rather have come down from his throne than have allowed his subjects to be legally shot by Russians and Prussians.

M. de Rayneval says, " The Holy Father has never failed to mitigate the severity of judgments."

I want to know in what way he has been enabled to mitigate these Austrian fusillades. Perhaps he has suggested a coating of soft cotton for the bullets.

CHAPTER XIV.

THE IMPUNITY OF REAL CRIME.

The Roman State is the most radically Catholic in Europe, seeing that it is governed by the Vicar of Jesus Christ himself. It is also the most fertile in crimes of every description, and above all, of violent crimes. So remarkable a contrast cannot escape observation. It is pointed out daily. Conclusions unfavorable to Catholicism have even been drawn from it; but this is a mistake. Let us not set down to religion that which is the necessary consequence of a particular form of government.

The Papacy has its root in Heaven, not in the country. It is not the Italian people who ask for a Pope,—it is Heaven that chooses him, the Sacred College that nominates him, diplomacy that maintains him, and the French army that imposes him upon the nation. The Sovereign Pontiff and his staff constitute a foreign body, introduced into Italy like a thorn into a woodcutter's foot.

What is the mission of the Pontifical Government? To what end did Europe bring Pius IX. from Gaeta to re-establish him at the Vatican? Was it for the sake of giving three millions of men an active and vigorous overseer? The merest brigadier of gendarmerie would have done the work better. No; it was in order that the Head of the Church might preside over the interests of religion from the elevation of a throne, and that the Vicar of Jesus Christ might be surrounded with royal splendour. The three millions of men who dwell in his States are appointed by Europe to defray the expenses of his court. In point of fact, we have given them to the Pope, not the Pope to them.

On this understanding, the Pope's first duty is to say Mass at St. Peter's for 139,000,000 of Roman Catholics; his second is to make a dignified appearance, to receive company, to wear a crown, and to take care it does not fall off his head. But it is a matter of perfect indifference to him that his subjects brawl, rob, or murder one another, so long as they don't attack either his Church or his government.

If we examine the question of the distribution of punishments in the Papal States from this point of view, we shall see that papal justice never strikes at random.

The most unpardonable crimes in the eyes of the clergy are those which are offensive to Heaven. Rome punishes sins. The tribunal of the Vicariate sends a blasphemer to the galleys, and claps into goal the silly fellow who refuses to take the Communion at Easter. Surely nobody will charge the Head of the Church with neglecting his duty.

I have told you how the Pope defends and will continue to defend his crown, and I have no fear of your charging him with weakness. If Europe ventured to allege that he suffers the throne on which it has placed him to be shaken, the answer would be a list of the political exiles and the prisoners of state, present and past—the living and the dead.

But the crimes and offences of which the natives are guilty towards one another affect the Pope and his Cardinals very remotely. What matters it to the successors of the Apostles that a few workmen and peasants should cut one another's throats after Sunday Vespers? There will always be enough of them left to pay the taxes.

The people of Rome have long contracted some very bad

habits. They frequent taverns and wine-shops, and they quarrel over their liquor; the word and the blow of other people is with them the word and the knife. The rural population are as bad as the townspeople. Quarrels between neighbours and relatives are submitted to the adjudication of cold steel. Of course they would do better to go before the nearest magistrate; but justice is slow in the States of the Church; lawsuits cost money, and bribery is the order of the day; the judges are either fools or knaves. So out with the knife! its decisions are swift and sure. Giacomo is down: 'tis clear he was in the wrong. Nicolo is unmolested: he must have been in the right. This little drama is performed more than four times a day in the Papal States, as is proved by the Government statistics of 1853. It is a great misfortune for the country, and a serious danger for Europe. The school of the knife, founded at Rome, establishes branches in foreign lands. We have seen the holiest interests of civilization placed under the knife, and all the honest people in the world, the Pope himself included, shuddered at the sight.

It would cost his Holiness very little trouble to snatch the knife from the hands of his subjects. We don't ask him to begin over again the education of his people, which would take time, or even to increase the attractions of civil justice, so as to substitute litigants for assassins. All we require of him is, that he should allow criminal justice to dispose of some few of the worst characters who throng to these evil haunts. But this very natural remedy would be utterly repugnant to his notions. The tavern assassin is seldom a foe to the Government.

Not that the Pope absolutely refuses to let assassins be pursued; that would be opposed to the practice of all civilized countries. But he takes care that they shall always get a good start of their pursuers. If they reach the banks of a river the pursuit ceases, lest they should jump into the water and be drowned without confession and absolution. If they seize hold of the skirts of a Capuchin Friar—they are saved. If they get into a church, a convent, or a hospital—saved again. If they do but set foot upon an ecclesiastical domain, or upon a clerical property (of which there is to the amount of £20,000,000 in the country), justice stands still, and lets them move on. A word from the Pope would reform this abuse of the right of asylum, which is a standing insult to civilization. On the contrary, he carefully preserves it, in order to show that the privileges of the Church are above the interests of humanity. This is both consistent and legal.

Should the police get hold of a murderer by accident, and quite unintentionally, he is brought up for trial. Witnesses of the crime are sought, but never found. A citizen would consider himself dishonoured if he were to give up his comrade to the natural enemy of the nation. The murdered man himself, if he could be brought to life, would swear he had seen nothing of the affair. The Government is not strong enough to force the witnesses to say what they know, or to protect them against the consequences of their depositions. This is why the most flagrant crime can never be proved in the courts of justice.

Supposing even that a murderer lets himself be taken, that witnesses give evidence against him, and that the crime be proved, even then the tribunal hesitates to pronounce the sentence of death.

The shedding of blood—legally—saddens a people; the Government has no fault to find with the murderer, so he is sent to the galleys. He is pretty comfortable there; public consideration follows him; sooner or later he is certain to be pardoned, because the Pope, utterly indifferent to his crime, finds it more profitable, and less expensive, to turn him loose than to keep him.

Put the worst possible case. Imagine a crime so glaring, so monstrous, so revolting, that the judges, who happen to be the least interested in the question, have been compelled to condemn the criminal to death. You probably imagine that, for example's sake, he will be executed while his crime is yet fresh in the popular recollection. Nothing of the sort. He is cast into a dungeon and forgotten; they think it probable he will die naturally there. In the month of July, 1858, the prison of the small town of Viterbo contained twenty-two criminals condemned to death, who were singing psalms while waiting for the executioner.

At length this functionary arrives; he selects one out of the lot and decapitates him. The populace is moved to compassion. Tears are shed, and the spectators cry out with one accord, "*Poveretto!*" The fact is, his crime is ten years old. Nobody recollects what it was. He has expiated it by ten years of penitence. Ten years ago his execution would have conveyed a striking moral lesson.

So much for the severity of penal justice. You would laugh if I were to speak of its leniency. The Duke Sforza Cesarini murders one of his servants for some act of personal disrespect. For example's sake, the Pope condemns him to a month's retirement in a convent.

Ah! if any sacrilegious hand were laid upon the holy ark; if a priest were to be slain, a Cardinal only threatened, then would there be neither asylum, nor galleys, nor clemency, nor delay. Thirty years ago the murderer of a priest was hewn in pieces in the Piazza del Popolo. More recently, as we have seen, the idiot who brandished his fork in the face of Cardinal Antonelli, was beheaded.

It is with highway robbery as with murder. I am induced to believe that the Pontifical court would not wage a very fierce war with the brigands, if those gentry undertook to respect its money and despatches. The occasional stopping of a few travellers, the clearing out of a carriage, and even the pillaging a country house, are neither religious nor political scourges. The brigands are not likely to scale either Heaven or the Vatican.

Thus there is still good business to be done in this line, and particularly beyond the Apennines, in those provinces which Austria has disarmed and does not protect. The tribunal of Bologna faithfully described the state of the country in a sentence of the 16th of June, 1856.

"Of late years this province has been afflicted by innumerable crimes of all sorts: robbery, pillage, attacks upon houses, have occurred at all hours, and in all places. The numbers of the malefactors have been constantly increasing, as has their audacity, encouraged by impunity."

Nothing is changed since the tribunal of Bologna spoke so forcibly. Stories, as improbable as they are true, are daily related in the country. The illustrious Passatore, who seized the entire population of Forlimpopoli in the theatre, has left successors. The audacious brigands who robbed a diligence in the very streets of Bologna, a few paces from the Austrian barracks, have not yet wholly disappeared. In the course of a tour of some weeks on the shores of the Adriatic, I heard more than one disquieting report. Near Rimini the house of a landed proprietor was besieged by a little army. In one place, all the inmates of the goal walked off, arm-in-arm with the turnkeys; in another a diligence came to grief just outside the walls of a city. If any particular district was allowed to live in peace, it was because the inhabitants subscribed and paid a ransom to the brigands.

Five times a week I used to meet the pontifical courier, escorted by an omnibus full of gendarmes, a sight which made me shrewdly suspect the country was not quite safe.

But if the Government is too weak or too careless to undertake an expedition against brigandage, and to purge the country thoroughly, it sometimes avenges its insulted authority and its stolen money. When by chance the Judges of Instruction are sent into the field, they do not trifle with their work. Not only do they press the prisoners to confess their crimes, but they press them in a thumbscrew! The tribunal of Bologna confessed this fact, with compunction, in 1856, alluding to the measures employed as *violenti e feroci.*

But simple theft, innocent theft, the petty larceny of snuff-boxes and pocket-handkerchiefs, the theft which seeks a modest alms in a neighbour's pocket, is tolerated as paternally as mendicity. Official statistics give the number of the beggars in Rome, I believe, somewhat under the mark; it is a pity they fail to give the number of pickpockets, who swarm through the city; this might easily have been done, as their names are all known to the authorities. No attempt is made to interfere with their operations: the foreign visitors are rich enough to pay this small tax in favour of the national industry; besides, it is not likely the pickpockets will ever make an attempt upon the Pope's pocket-handkerchief.

A Frenchman once caught hold of an elegantly dressed gentleman in the act of snatching away his watch; he took him to the nearest post, and placed him in the charge of the sergeant. "I believe your statement," said the official, "for I know the man well, and so would you, if you were not very new to the country. He is a Lombard; but if we were to arrest all his fellows, our prisons would never be

6*

half large enough. Be off, my fine fellow, and take better care for the future!"

Another foreigner was robbed in the Corso at midnight, on his return from the theatre. All the consolation he got from the magistrate to whom he complained was, "Sir, you were out at an hour when all honest people should be in bed."

A traveller was stopped between Rome and Civita Vecchia, and robbed of all the money he had about him. When he reached Palo, he laid his complaint before the political functionary who taxes travellers for the trouble of fumbling with their passports. The observation of this worthy man was, "What can you expect? the people are so very poor!"

On the eve of the grand fêtes, however, all the riffraff are bound to go to prison, lest the religious ceremonies should be disturbed by evil-doers. They go of their own accord, as an amicable concession to a paternal government: and if any professional thief were by chance to absent himself, he would be politely sent for about midnight. But in spite even of these vigilant measures, it is seldom that a Holy Week goes by without a watch or two going astray; and to any complaint the police would be sure to reply: "You must not blame us; we have taken every necessary precaution against such accidents. We have got all the thieves who are inscribed on our books under lock and key. For any new comers we are not responsible."

The following incident occurred while I was at Rome; it serves to illustrate the pleasing fraternal tie which unites the magistrates with the thieves.

A former secretary to Monsignor Vardi, by name Berti, had a gold snuff-box, which he prized highly, it having been given him by his master. One day, crossing the Forum, he took out his snuff-box, just in front of the temple of Antoninus and Faustina, and solaced himself with a pinch of the contents. The incautious act had been marked by one of the pets of the police. He had hardly returned the box to his pocket ere he was hustled by some quoit-players, and knocked down. It is needless to add, that, when he got up, the precious snuff-box was gone.

He mentioned the affair to a judge of his acquaintance, who at once told him to set his mind at rest, adding, "Pass through the Forum again to-morrow. Ask for *Antonio;* anybody will point him out to you; tell him you come from me, and mention what you have lost. He will put you in the way of getting it back."

Berti did as he was desired; Antonio was soon found. He smiled meaningly when the judge's name was mentioned, protested that he could refuse him nothing, and immediately called out, "Eh! Giacomo!"

Another bandit came out of the ruins, and ran up to his chief.

"Who was on duty yesterday?" asked Antonio.

"Pepe."

"Is he here?"

"No, he made a good day of it yesterday. He's drinking it out."

"I can do nothing for your Excellency to-day," said Antonio. "Come here to-morrow at the same hour, and I think you'll have reason to be satisfied."

Berti was punctual to the appointment. Signor Antonio, for fear of being swindled, asked for an accurate description of the missing article. This having been given, he at once produced the snuff-box. "Your Excellency will please to pay me two scudi," he said; "I should have charged you four, but that you are recommended to me by a magistrate whom I particularly esteem."

It would appear that all the Roman magistrates are not equally estimable; at least to judge from what happened to the Marquis de Sesmaisons. He was robbed of half-a-dozen silver spoons and forks. He imprudently lodged a complaint with the authorities. Being asked for an exact description of the stolen articles, he sent the remaining half-dozen to speak for themselves to the magistrate who had charge of the affair. It is chronicled that he never again saw either the first or the second half-dozen!

The malversations of public functionaries are tolerated so long as they do not directly touch the higher powers. Officials of every degree hold out their hands for a present. The Government rather encourages the system than the reverse. It is just so much knocked off the salaries.

The Government even overlooks embezzlement of public money, provided the guilty party be an ecclesiastic, or well affected to the present order of things. The errors of friends are judged *en famille*. If a Prelate make a mistake, he is reprimanded, and dismissed, which means that his situation is changed for a better one.

Monsignor N— gets the holy house of Loretto into financial trouble. The consequence is that Monsignor N— is removed to Rome, and placed at the head of the hospital of the Santo Spirito. Probably this is done because the latter establishment is richer and more difficult to get into financial trouble than the holy house of Loretto.

Monsignor A— was an Auditor of the Rota, and made a bad judge. He was made a Prefect of Bologna. He failed to give satisfaction at Bologna, and was made a Minister, and still remains so.

If occasionally officials of a certain rank are punished, if even the law is put in force against them with unusual vigour, rest assured the public interest has no part in the business. The real springs of action are to be sought elsewhere. Take as an example the Campana affair, which created such a sensation in 1858.

This unfortunate Marquis succeeded his father and his grandfather as Director of the Monte di Pietà, or public pawnbroking establishment. His office placed him immediately under the control of the Finance Minister. It was that Minister's duty to overlook his acts, and to prevent him from going wrong.

Campana went curiosity mad. The passion of collecting, which has proved the ruin of so many well-meaning people, drove him to his destruction. He bought pictures, marbles, bronzes, Etruscan vases. He heaped gallery on gallery. He bought at random everything that was offered to him. Rome never had such a terrible buyer. He bought as people drink, or take snuff, or smoke opium. When he had no more money of his own left to buy with, he began to think of a loan. The coffers of the Monte di Pietà were at hand: he would borrow of himself, upon the security of his collection. The Finance Minister Galli offered no difficulties. Campana was in favour at Court, esteemed by the Pope, liked by the Cardinals; his principles were known, he had proved his devotion to those in power. The Government never refuses its friends anything. In short Campana was allowed to lend himself £4,000, for which he gave security to a much larger amount.

But the order by which the Minister gave him permission to draw from the coffers of the Monte di Pietà was so loosely drawn up, that he was enabled to take, without any fresh authority, a trifle of something like £106,000. This he took between the 12th of April, 1854, and the 1st of December 1856, a period of nineteen months and a half.

There was no concealment in the transaction; it certainly was irregular, but it was not clandestine. Campana paid himself the interest of the money he had lent himself. In 1856 he was paternally reprimanded. He received a gentle rap over the knuckles, but there was not the least idea of tying his hands. He stood well at Court.

The unfortunate man still went on borrowing. They had not even taken the precaution to close his coffers against himself. Between the 1st of December, 1856, and the 7th of November, 1857, he took a further sum of about £103,000. But he gave grand parties; the Cardinals adored him; testimonies of satisfaction poured in upon him from all sides.

The real truth is that a national pawnbroking establishment is of no use to the Church, it is only required for the nation. Campana might have borrowed the very walls of the building, without the Pontifical Court meddling in the matter.

Unluckily for him, the time came when it answered the purpose of Antonelli to send him to the galleys. This great statesman had three objects to gain by such a course. Firstly, he would stop the mouth of diplomacy, and silence the foreign press, which both charged the Pope with tolerating an abuse. Secondly, he would humiliate one of those laymen who take the liberty to rise in the world without wearing violet hose. Lastly, he should be able to bestow Campana's place upon one of his brothers, the worthy and interesting Filippo Antonelli.

He took a long time to mature his scheme, and laid his train silently and secretly. He is not a man to take any step inconsiderately. While Campana was going and coming, and giving dinners, and buying more statues, in blissful ignorance of the lowering storm, the Cardinal negotiated a loan at Rothschild's, made arrangements to cover the deficit, and instructed the Procuratore Fiscale to draw up an indictment for peculation.

The accusation fell like a thunderbolt upon the poor Marquis. From his palace to his prison was but a step. As he entered there, he rubbed his eyes, and asked himself, ingenuously enough, whether this move was not all a horrible dream. He would have laughed at any one who had told him he was seriously in danger. He charged with peculation! Out upon it! Peculation meant the clandestine application by a public officer of public funds to his private profit: whereas he had taken nothing clandestinely, and was ruined root and branch. So he quietly occupied himself in his prison by writing sonnets, and when an artist came to pay him a visit, he gave him an order for a new work.

In spite of the eloquent defence made in his behalf by a young advocate, the tribunal condemned him to twenty years' hard labour. At this rate, the Minister who had allowed him to borrow the money should certainly have been beheaded. But the lambs of the clergy don't eat one another.

The advocate who had defended Campana was punished for having pleaded too eloquently, by being forbidden to practise in Court for three months.

You may imagine that this cruel sentence cast a stigma upon Campana. Not a bit of it. The people, who have often experienced his generosity, regard him as a martyr. The middle class despises him much less than it does many a yet unpunished functionary. His old friends of the nobility and of the Sacred College often shake him by the hand. I have known Cardinal Tosti, at once his gaoler and his friend, let him have the use of his private kitchen.

Condemnations are a dishonour only in countries where the judges are honoured. All the world knows that the pontifical magistrates are not instruments of justice, but tools of power.

CHAPTER XV.

TOLERANCE.

If crimes against Heaven are those which the Church forgives the least, every man who is not even nominally a Catholic, is of course in the eyes of the Pope a rogue and a half.

These criminals are very numerous: the geographer Balbi enumerates some six hundred millions of them on the surface of the globe. The Pope continues to damn them all conformably with the tradition of the Church; but he has given up levying armies to make war upon them here below.

Things are improved when we daily find the Head of the Roman Catholic Church in friendly intercourse with the foes of his religion. He partakes of the liberality of a Mussulman Prince; he receives a schismatic Empress as a loving father; he converses familiarly with a Queen who has abjured Catholicism to marry a Protestant; he receives with distinction the aristocracy of the New Jerusalem; he sends his Major-domo to attend upon a young heretic prince* travelling *incognito*. I hardly know whether Gregory VII. would approve this tolerance; nor can I tell how it is judged in the other world by the instigators of the Crusades, or by the

* H.R.H. the Prince of Wales.

advisers of the Massacre of St. Bartholomew. For my own part, I should award it unbounded praise, if I could believe it took its source in a spirit of enlightenment and Christian charity. I should regard it differently, if I thought it was to be traced to calculations of policy and interest.

The difficulty is to penetrate the secret thoughts of the Sovereign Pontiff; to find a key to the real motive of his tolerance. Natural mildness and interested mildness resemble each other in their effects, but differ widely in their causes. When the Pope and the Cardinals overwhelm M. de Rothschild with assurances of their highest consideration, are we to conclude that an Israelite is equal to a Roman Catholic in their eyes, as he is in yours or mine? Or are we to conclude that they deem it expedient to mask their real sentiments because M. de Rothschild has millions to spare?

This delicate problem is not difficult to solve. We have but to seek out a Jew in Rome who is *not* the possessor of millions, and to ask him how he is considered and treated by the Popes. If the Government really make no difference between this citizen who is a Jew, and another who is a Catholic, I will say the Popes have become tolerant in earnest. If, on the contrary, we find that the administration accords this poor Jew a social position somewhere between man and the dog, then I am bound to set down the fine speeches made to M. de Rothschild, as proceeding from calculations of interest, and as inferring a sacrifice of dignity.

Now mark, and judge for yourselves. There were Jews in Italy before there were Christians in the world. Roman polytheism, which tolerated everything except the kicks administered by Polyeucte to the statue of Jupiter, gave a place to the God of Israel. Afterwards came the Christians, and they were tolerated till they conspired against the laws They were often confounded with the Jews, because they came from the same corner of the East. Christianity increased by means of pious conspiracies; enrolled slaves braved their masters, and became master in its turn. I don't blame it for practising reprisals, and cutting the pagans' throats; but in common justice it has killed too many Jews.

Not at Rome. The Popes kept a specimen of the accursed race to bring before God at the last judgment. The Scripture had warned the Jews that they should live miserably till the consummation of time. The Church, ever mindful of prophecy, undertook to keep them alive and miserable. She made enclosures for them, as we do in our *Jardin des Plantes* for rare animals. At first they were folded in the valley of Egeria, then they were penned in the Trastevere, and finally cribbed in the Ghetto. In the daytime they were allowed to go about the city, that the people might see what a dirty, degraded being a man is when he does not happen to be a Christian; but when night came they were put under lock and key. The Ghetto used to close just as the Faithful were on their way to damnation at the theatre.

On tho occasion of certain solemnities the Municipal Council of Rome amused the populace with *Jew races.*

When modern philosophy had somewhat softened Catholic manners, horses were substituted for Jews. The Senator of the city used annually to administer to them an official kick in the seat of honour: which token of respect they acknowledged by a payment of 800 scudi. At every accession of a Pope, they were obliged to range themselves under the Arch of Titus, and to offer the new Pontiff a Bible, in return for which he addressed to them an insulting observation.

They paid a perpetual annuity of 450 scudi to the heirs of a renegade who had abused them. They paid the salary of a preacher charged to work at their conversion every Saturday, and if they stayed away from the sermon they were fined. But they paid no taxes in the strict sense of the word, because they were not citizens. The law regarded them in the light of travellers at an inn. The license to dwell in Rome was provisional, and for many centuries it was renewed every year. Not only were they without any political rights, but they were deprived of even the most elementary civil rights. They could neither possess property, nor engage in manufactures, nor cultivate the soil: they lived by botching and brokage. How they lived at all surprises me. Want, filth, and the infected atmosphere of their dens, had impoverished their blood, made them wan and haggard, and stamped disgrace upon their looks. Some of them scarcely retained the semblance of humanity. They might have been taken for brutes; yet they were notoriously intelligent, apt at business, resigned to their lot, good-tempered, kind-hearted, devoted to their families, and irreproachable in their general conduct.

I need not add that the Roman rabble, bettering the instruction of Catholic monks, spurned them, reviled them, and robbed them. The law forbade Christians to hold converse with them, but to steal anything from them was a work of grace.

The law did not absolutely sanction the murder of a Jew; but the tribunals regarded the murderer of a man in a different light from the murderer of a Jew. Mark the line of pleading that follows.

"Why, Gentlemen, does the law severely punish murderers, and sometimes go the length of inflicting upon them the penalty of death? Because he who murders a Christian murders at once a body and a soul. He sends before the Sovereign Judge a being who is ill-prepared, who has not received absolution, and who falls straight into hell—or, at the very least, into purgatory. This is why murder—I mean the murder of a Christian—cannot be too severely punished. But as for us (counsel and client), what have we killed? Nothing, Gentlemen, absolutely nothing but a wretched Jew, predestined for damnation. You know the obstinacy of his race, and you know that if he had been allowed a hundred years for his conversion, he would have died like a brute, without confession. I admit that we have advanced by some years the maturity of celestial justice; we have hastened a little for him an eternity of torture which sooner or later must inevitably have been his lot. But be indulgent, Gentlemen, towards so venial an offence, and reserve your severity for those who attempt the life and salvation of a Christian!"

This speech would be nonsense at Paris. It was sound logic at Rome, and, thanks to it, the murderer got off with a few months' imprisonment.

You will ask why the Jews have not fled a hundred leagues from this Slough of Despond. The answer is, because they were born there. Moreover, the taxation is light, and rent is moderate. Add that, when famine has been in the land, or the inundations of the Tiber have spread ruin and devastation around, the scornful charity of the Popes has flung them some bones to gnaw. Then again, travelling costs money, and passports are not to be had for the asking in Rome.

But if, by some miracle of industry, one of these unfortunate children of Israel has managed to accumulate a little money, his first thought has been to place his family beyond the reach of the insults of the Ghetto. He has realized his little fortune, and has gone to seek liberty and consideration in some less Catholic country. This accounts for the fact that the Ghetto was no richer at the accession of Pius IX. than it was in the worst days of the Middle Ages.

History has made haste to write in letters of gold all the good deeds of the reigning Pope, and, above all, the enfranchisement of the Jews.

Pius IX. has removed the gates of the Ghetto. He allows the Jews to go about by night as well as by day, and to live where they like. He has exempted them from the municipal kick and the 800 scudi which it cost them. He has closed the little church where these poor people were catechized every Saturday, against their will, and at their own expense. His accession may be regarded, then, as an era of deliverance for the people of Israel who have set up their tents in Rome.

Europe, which sees things from afar, naturally supposes that under so tolerant a sway as that of Pius IX., Jews have thronged from all parts of the world into the Papal States. But see how paradoxical a science is that of statistics. From it we learn that in 1842, under Gregory XVI., during the captivity of Babylon, the little kingdom of the Pope contained 12,700 Jews. We further learn that in 1853, in the teeth of such reforms, such a shower of benefits, such justice, and such tolerance, the Israelites in the kingdom were reduced to 9,237. In other words, 3,463 Jews—more than a quarter of the Jewish population—had withdrawn from the paternal action of the Holy Father.

Either this people is very ungrateful, or we don't know the whole state of the case.

While I was at Rome, I had secret inquiries on the subject made of two notables of the Ghetto. When the poor people heard the object I had in view in my inquiries, they expressed great alarm. "For Heaven's sake don't pity us!" they cried. "Let not the outer world learn through your book that we are unfortunate—that the Pope shows by his acts how bitterly he regrets the benefits conferred upon us in 1847—that the Ghetto is closed by doors invisible, but impassable—and that our condition is worse than ever! All you say in our favour will turn against us, and that which you intend for our good will do us infinite harm."

This is all the information I could obtain as to the treatment of this persecuted people. It is little enough, but it is something. I found that their Ghetto, in which some hidden power keeps them shut up just as in past times, was the foulest and most neglected quarter of the city, whence I concluded that nothing was done for them by the municipality. I learnt that neither the Pope, nor the Cardinals, nor the Bishops, nor the least of the Prelates, could set foot on this accursed ground without contracting a moral stain—the custom of Rome forbids it: and I thought of those Indian Pariahs whom a Brahmin cannot touch without losing caste. I learnt that the lowest places in the lowest of the public offices were inaccessible to Jews, neither more nor less than they would be to animals. A child of Israel might as well apply for the place of a copying-clerk at Rome as one of the giraffes in the Jardin des Plantes for the post of a Sous-Préfet. I ascertained that none of them are or can be landowners, a fact which satisfies me that Pius IX. has not yet come quite to regard them as men. If one of their tribe cultivates another man's field, it is by smuggling himself into the occupation under a borrowed name; as though the sweat of a Jew dishonoured the earth. Manufactures are forbidden them, as of old; not being of the nation, they might injure the national industry. To conclude, I have observed them myself as they stood on the thresholds of their miserable shops, and I can assure you they do not resemble a people freed from oppression. The seal of pontifical reprobation is not removed from their foreheads. If, as history pretends, they had been liberated for the last twelve years, some sign of freedom would be perceptible on their countenances.

I am willing to admit that, at the commencement of his reign, Pius IX. experienced a generous impulse. But this is a country in which good is only done by immense efforts, while evil occurs naturally. I would liken it to a waggon being drawn up a steep mountain ascent. The joint efforts of four stout bullocks are required to drag it forward: it runs backwards by itself.

Were I to tell you all that M. de Rothschild has done for his co-religionists at Rome, you would be astounded. Not only are they supported at his expense, but he never concludes a transaction with the Pope without introducing into it a secret article or two in their favour. And still the waggon goes backwards.

The French occupation might be beneficial to the Jews. Our officers are not wanting in good will; but the bad will of the priests neutralizes their efforts. By way of illustrating the operation of these two influences, I will relate a little incident which recently occurred.

An Israelite of Rome had hired some land in defiance of the law, under the name of a Christian. As everybody knew that the Jew was the real farmer, he was robbed right and left in the most unscrupulous manner, merely because he *was* a Jew. The poor man, foreseeing that before rent-day he should be completely ruined, applied for leave to have a guard sworn to protect his property. The authorities replied that under no pretext should a Christian be sworn in the service of a Jew. Disappointed in his application, he mentioned the fact to some French officers, and asked for the assistance of the French Commander-in-Chief. It was readily promised by M. de Goyon, one of the kindest-hearted men alive, who undertook moreover to apply personally to the Cardinal in the matter. The reply he received from his Eminence was, "What you ask is nothing short of an impossibility. Nevertheless, as the Government of the Holy Father is unable to refuse you anything, we will do it. Not only shall your Jew have a sworn guard, but out of our affection for you, we will select him ourselves."

Delighted at having done a good action, the General warmly thanked the Cardinal, and departed. Three months elapsed, and still no sworn guard made his appearance at the Jew's farm. The poor fellow, robbed more than ever, timidly applied again to the General, who once more took the field in his behalf. This time, in order to make the matter sure, he would not leave the Cardinal till he held in his own hand the permission, duly filled up and signed. The delighted Jew shed tears of gratitude as he read to his family the thrice-blessed name of the guard assigned to him. The name was that of a man who had disappeared six years back, and never been heard of since.

When the French officers next met the Jew, they asked him whether he was pleased with his sworn guard. He dared not say that he had no guard: the police had forbidden him to complain.

The Jews of Rome are the most unfortunate in the Papal States. The vicinity of the Vatican is as fatal to them as to the Christians. Far from the seat of government, beyond the Apennines, they are less poor, less oppressed, and less despised. The Israelitish population of Ancona is really a fine race.

It is not to be inferred from this that the agents of the

Pope become converts to tolerance by crossing the Apennines.

It is not a year since the Archbishop of Bologna confiscated the boy Mortara for the good of the Convent of the Neophytes.

Only two years ago the Prefect of Ancona revived the old law, which forbids Christians to converse publicly with Jews.

It is not ten years since a merchant of considerable fortune, named P. Cadova, was deprived of his wife and children by means as remarkable as those employed in the case of young Mortara, although the affair created less sensation at the time.

M. P. Cadova lived at Cento, in the province of Ferrara. He had a pretty wife, and two children. His wife was seduced by one of his clerks, who was a Catholic. The intrigue being discovered, the clerk was driven from the house. The faithless wife soon joined her lover at Bologna, and took her children with her.

The Jew applied to the courts of law to assist him in taking the children from the adulteress.

The answer he received to his application was, that his wife and children had all three embraced Christianity, and had consequently ceased to be his family.

The Courts further decreed that he should pay an annual income for their support.

On this income the adulterous clerk also subsists.

Some months later Monsignore Oppiszoni, Archbishop of Bologna, himself celebrated the marriage of M. P. Cadova's wife and M. P. Cadova's ex-clerk.

Of course, you'll say, P. Cadova was dead. Not a bit of it. He was alive, and as well as a broken-hearted man could be. The Church, then, winked at a case of bigamy? Not so. In the States of the Church a woman may be married at the same time to a Jew and a Catholic, without being a bigamist, because in the States of the Church a Jew is not a man.

CHAPTER XVI.

EDUCATION OF THE PEOPLE.

All the world knows, and says over and over again, that education is less advanced in the Papal States than in any country in Europe. It is a source of universal regret that the nation which is, perhaps, of all others the most intelligent by God's grace, should be the most ignorant by the will of priests. This people has been compared to a thorough-bred horse, reduced from racing to walking blindfolded, round and round, grinding corn.

But people who talk thus take a partial view of the question. They don't, or they won't, see how entirely the development of public ignorance is in conformity with the principles of the Church, and how favourable it is to the maintenance of priestly government.

Religions are founded, not upon knowledge, or science, but upon faith, or, as some term it, credulity. People have agreed to describe as an "act of faith" the operation of closing one's eyes in order to see better. It is by walking with faith,—in other words, with one's eyes shut,—that the gates of Paradise are reached. If we could take from afar the census of that locality, we should find there more of the illiterate than of the learned. A child that knows the catechism by heart is more pleasing in the sight of Heaven than all the five classes of the Institute. The Church will never hesitate between an astronomer and a Capuchin friar. Knowledge is full of dangers. Not only does it puff up the heart of man, but it often shatters by the force of reasoning the best-constructed fables. Knowledge has made terrible havoc in the Roman Catholic Church during the last two or three hundred years. Who can tell how many souls have been cast into hell through the invention of printing.

Applied to the industrial pursuits of this sublunary sphere, science engenders riches, luxury, pleasure, health, and a thousand similar scourges, which tend to draw us away from salvation. Science cures even those irreligious maladies wherein religion used to recognize the finger of God. It no longer permits the sinner to make himself a purgatory here below. There is danger lest it should one of these days render man's terrestrial abode so blessed, that he may conceive an antipathy to Heaven. The Church, having the mission to conduct us to that eternal felicity which is the sole end of human existence, is bound to discourage our dealings with science. The utmost she can venture to do is to let a select number of her most trustworthy servants have free access to it, in order that the enemies of the faith may find somebody whom they can speak to.

This is why I undertake to show you in Rome a dozen men of high literary and scientific acquirements, to a hundred thousand who don't know their A B C.

The Church is but the more flourishing for it, and the State by no means the less so. The true shepherds of peoples, they who feed the sheep for the sake of selling the wool and the skins, do not want them to know too much. The mere fact of a man's being able to read makes him wish to meddle with everything. The custom-house may be made to keep him from reading dangerous books, but he'll be sure to take the change out of the laws of the kingdom. He'll begin to inquire whether they are good or bad, whether they accord with or contradict one another, whether they are obeyed or broken. No sooner can he calculate without the help of his fingers, than he'll want to look up the figures of the Budget. But if he has reached the culminating point of knowing how to use his pen, the sight of the smallest bit of paper will give him a sort of political itching. He will experience an uncontrollable desire to express his sentiments as a man and a citizen, by voting for one representative, and against another. And, gracious goodness! what will become of us if the refractory sheep should get as high as the generalities of history, or the speculations of philosophy?—if he should begin to stir important questions, to inquire into great truths, to refute sophisms, to point out abuses, to demand rights? The shepherd's occupation is assuredly not all roses from the day he finds it necessary to muzzle his flock.

Sovereigns who are not Popes have nothing to fear from the progress of enlightenment, for their interest does not lie in the fabrication of saints, but in the making of men. In France, England, Piedmont, and some other countries, the Governments urge, or even oblige the people to seek instruction. This is because a power which is based on reason has no fear of being discussed. Because the acts of a really national administration have no reason to dread the inquiry of the nation. Because it is not only a nobler but an easier task to govern reflecting beings than mere brutes,—always supposing the Government to be in the right. Because education softens men's manners, eradicates their evil instincts, reduces the average of crime, and simplifies the policeman's duty. Because science applied to manufactures will, in a few years, increase a hundredfold the prosperity of the nation, the wealth of the State, and the resources of power.

Because the discoveries of pure science, good books, and all the higher productions of the mind, even when they are not sources of material profit, are an honour to a country, the splendour of an age, and the glory of a Sovereign.

All the princes in Europe, with the single exception of the Pope, limit their views to the things of the earth; and they do wisely. Without raising a doubt as to a future existence in another and a better world, they govern their subjects only with regard to this life. They seek to obtain for them all the happiness of which man is capable here below; they labour to render him as perfect as he can be as long as he retains this poor "mortal coil." We should regard them as *mauvais plaisants* if they were to think it their duty to make for us the trials of Job, while showing us a future prospect of eternal bliss.

But the fact is that our emperors and kings and lay sovereigns are men with wives and children, personally interested in the education of the rising generation, and the future of their people. A good Pope, on the contrary, has no other object but to gain Heaven himself, and to drag up a hundred and thirty millions of men after him. Thus it is that his subjects can with an ill grace ask of him those temporal advantages which secular princes feel bound to offer their subjects spontaneously.

In the Papal States the schools for the lower classes are both few and far between. The government does nothing to increase either their number or their usefulness, the parishes being obliged to maintain them; and even this source is sometimes cut off, for not unfrequently the minister disallows this heading in the municipal budget, and pockets the money himself. In addition to this, secondary teaching, excepting in the colleges, exists but in name; and I should advise any father who wishes his son's education to extend beyond the catechism, to send him into Piedmont.

But on the other hand, I am bound to urge in the Pope's behalf that the colleges are numerous, well endowed, and provided with ample means for turning out mediocre priests. The monasteries devote themselves to the education of little monks. They are taught from an early age to hold a wax taper, wear a frock, cast down their eyes, and chant in Latin. If you wish to admire the foresight of the Church, you should see the procession of Corpus Christi day. All the convents walk in line one after the other, and each has its live nursery of little shavelings. Their bright Italian eyes, sparkling with intelligence, and their handsome open countenances, form a curious contrast with the stolid and hypocritical masks worn by their superiors. At one glance you behold the opening flowers and the ripe fruit of religion,—the present and the future. You think within yourselves that, in default of a miracle, the cherubs before you will ere long be turned into mummies. However, you console yourselves for the anticipated metamorphosis by the reflection that the salvation of the monklings is assured.

All the Pope's subjects would be sure of getting to Heaven if they could all enter the cloisters; but then the world would come to an end too soon. The Pope does his best to bring them near this state of monastic and ecclesiastical perfection. Students are dressed like priests, and corpses also are arrayed in a sort of religious costume. The Brethren of the Christian Doctrine were thought dangerous because they dressed their little boys in caps, tunics, and belts; so the Pope forbade them to go on teaching young Rome. The Bolognese (beyond the Apennines) founded by subscription asylums under the direction of lay female teachers. The clergy make most praiseworthy efforts to reform such an abuse.

There is not a law, not a regulation, not a deed nor a word of the higher powers, which does not tend to the edification of the people, and to urge them on heavenward

Enter this church. A monk is preaching with fierce gesticulations. He is not in the pulpit, but he stands about twenty paces from it, on a plank hastily flung across trestles. Don't be afraid of his treating a question of temporal ethics after the fashion of our worldly preachers. He is dogmatically and furiously descanting on the Immaculate Conception, on fasting in Lent, on avoiding meat of a Friday, on the doctrine of the Trinity, on the special nature of hell-fire.

"Bethink you, my brethren, that if terrestrial fire, the fire created by God for your daily wants and your general use, can cause you such acute pain at the least contact with your flesh, how much more fierce and terrible must be that flame of hell-fire which ever devours without consuming those who . . . etc. etc." I spare you the rest.

Our sacred orators for the most part confine themselves to preaching on such subjects as fidelity, to wives; probity, to men; obedience, to children. They descend to a level with a lay congregation, and endeavour to sow, each according to his powers, a little virtue on earth. Verily, Roman eloquence cares very much for virtue! It is greatly troubled about the things of earth! It takes the people by the shoulders and forces them into the paths of devotion, which lead straight to Heaven. And it does its duty, according to the teachings of the Church.

Open one of the devotional books which are printed in the country. Here is one selected at random, 'The Life of St. Jacintha.' It lies on a young girl's work-table. A knitting-needle marks the place at which the gentle reader left off this morning. Let us turn to the passage. It is sure to be highly edifying.

"*Chapter V.—She casts from her heart all natural affection for her relations.*

"Knowing from the Redeemer himself that we ought not to love our relations more than God, and feeling herself naturally drawn towards hers, she feared lest such a love, although natural, if it should take root and grow in her heart, might in the course of time surpass or impede the love she owed to God, and render her unworthy of him. So she formed the very generous determination of casting from herself all affection for the persons of her blood.

"Resolved on conquering herself by this courageous determination, and on triumphing over opposing nature itself,—powerfully urged thereto by another word of Christ, who said that in order to go to him we must hate our relations, when the love we bear them stands in the way,—she went and solemnly performed a great act of renunciation before the altar of the most holy Sacrament. There, flinging herself on her knees, her heart kindling with an ardent flame of charity towards God, she offered up to Him all the natural affections of her heart, more especially those which she felt were the strongest within her for the nearest and dearest of her relations. In this heroic action she obtained the intervention of the most holy Virgin, as may be seen by a letter in her handwriting addressed to a regular priest, wherein she promises, by the aid of the holy Virgin, to attach herself no more either to her relations, or to any other earthly object. This renunciation was so resolutely courageous and so sincere that from that hour her brothers, sisters, nephews, and all her kindred became to her objects of total indifference; and she deemed herself thenceforth so much an orphan and alone in the world, that she was enabled to see and converse with her aforesaid relations when they came to see her at the convent, as if they were persons utterly unknown to her.

"She had made herself in Paradise an entirely spiritual family, selected from among the saints who had been the greatest sinners. Her father was St. Augustin; her mother St. Mary the Egyptian; her brother St. William the Hermit, ex-Duke of Aquitaine; her sister St. Margaret of Cortona; her uncle St. Peter, the Prince of the Apostles; her nephews the three children of the furnace of Babylon."

Now here is a book that you, probably, attribute to the monkish ages; a book expressing the isolated sentiments of a mind obscured by the gloom of the cloisters.

In order to convince you of your error, I will give you its title and date, and the opinion concerning it expressed by the rulers of Rome.

"Life of the Virgin Saint Jacintha Mariscotti, a professed Nun of the Third Order of the Seraphic Father St. Francis, written by the Father Flaminius Mary Hanibal of Latara, Brother Observant of the Order of the Minors. Rome, 1805. Published by Antonio Fulgoni, by permission of the Superiors.

"Approbation.—The book is to the glory and honour of the Catholic Religion and the illustrious Order of St. Francis, and to the spiritual profit of those persons who desire to enter into the way of perfection.

"Brother Thomas Mancini, of the Order of Preachers, Master, ex-Provincial, and Consultor of Sacred Rites.

"Imprimatur. Brother Thomas Vincent Pani, of the Order of Preachers, Master of the Sacred Apostolical Palace."

Now here we have a woman, a writer, a censor, and a Master of the Palace, who are ready to strangle the whole human race for the sake of hastening its arrival in Paradise. These people are only doing their duty.

Just look out into the street. Four men of different ages are kneeling in the mud before a Madonna, whining out prayers. Presently, fifteen or twenty others come upon you, chanting a canticle to the glory of Mary. Perhaps you think they are yielding to a natural inspiration, and freely working out their salvation. I thought so myself, till I was told that they were paid fifteen-pence for thus edifying the bystanders. This comedy in the open air is subsidized by the Government. And the Government does its duty.

The streets and roads swarm with beggars. Under lay governments the poor either receive succour in their own homes, or are admitted to houses of public charity; they are not allowed to obstruct the public thoroughfares, and tyrannize over the passengers. But we are in an ecclesiastical country. On the one hand, poverty is dear to God; on the other, alms-giving is a deed of piety. If the Pope could make one half of his subjects hold out their hands, and the other half put a halfpenny into each extended palm, he would effect the salvation of an entire people.

Mendicity, which lay sovereigns regard as an ugly sore in the State, to be healed, is tended and watered as a fair flower by a clerical government. Pray give something to yonder sham cripple; give to that cadger who pretends to have lost an arm; and be sure you don't forget that blind young man leaning on his father's arm! A medical man of my acquaintance offered yesterday to restore his sight, by operating for the cataract. The father cried aloud with indignant horror at the proposal; the boy is a fortune to him. Drop an alms for the son into the father's bowl; the Pope will let you into Paradise, of which he keeps the keys

The Romans themselves are not duped by their beggars. They are too sharp to be taken in by these swindlers in misery. Still they put their hands into their pockets; some from weakness or humanity, some from ostentation, some to gain Paradise. If you doubt my assertion, try an experiment which I once did, with considerable success. One night, between nine and ten o'clock, I begged all along the Corso. I was not disguised as a beggar. I was dressed as if I were on the Boulevards at Paris. Still, between the Piazza del Popolo and the Piazza di Venezia, I *made* sixty-three baiocchi (about three shillings). If I were to try the same joke at Paris, the *sergents-de-ville* would very properly think it their duty to walk me off to the nearest police-station. The Pontifical Government encourages mendicity by the protection of its agents, and recommends it by the example of its friars. The Pontifical Government does its duty.

Prostitution flourishes in Rome, and in all the large towns of the States of the Church. The police is too paternal to refuse the consolations of the flesh to three millions of persons out of whom five or six thousand have taken the vow of celibacy. But in proportion as it is indulgent to vice, it is severe in cases of scandal. It only allows light conduct in women when they are sheltered by the protection of a husband.* It casts the cloak of Japhet over the vices of

* Leo XII. (out of his excessive regard for the interests of morality) occasionally departed from this rule. The same motive caused him to be very fond of what the profane call "gossip." He had a habit, too, of ascertaining by ocular demonstration, whether any incidents of more than ordinary interest in domestic life were passing in the palaces of his noble, or the houses of his citizen subjects. His medium for the attainment of this end was a powerful telescope, placed at one of his upper windows! The principal minister to his gossiping propensities was one

the Romans, in order that the pleasures of one nation may not be a scandal to others. Rather than admit the existence of the evil, it refuses to place it under proper restraint: lay governments appear to sanction the social evil, when they place it under the control of the law. The clerical police is perfectly aware that its noble and wilful blindness exposes the health of an entire people to certain danger. But it rubs its hands at the reflection that the sinners are punished by the very sin itself. The clerical police does its duty.

Captain C......, a man of great learning, but doubtful morality, selected, of course, for the office of scandalous chronicler, from his experiences in what, in lay countries, the carnally-minded term "life." When, between his telescopic observations, and the reports of the Captain, the Sovereign Pontiff had accumulated the requisite amount of evidence against any offending party, the mode of procedure was sudden, swift, and sure, fully bearing out the Author's assertion that in Rome the will of an individual is a substitute for the law of the State. There was no nonsense about *Habeas Corpus*, or jury, or recorded judgment. The supposed delinquent was simply seized (usually in the dead of the night, to avoid scandal), and hurried off to durance vile, to undergo, as it was phrased, *prigione ed altre pene a nostro arbitrio.* One day C...... brought the Pope particulars of what was at once pronounced by his Holiness a most flagrant case. The wife of the highly respected and able *Avocato* B.......... (a stout lady of fifty), who was at the same time legal adviser to the French Embassy, was in the habit of driving out daily in the carriage, and by the side of the old bachelor Duke C.........., Exempt of the Noble Guard. The Papal decision on the case was instant. The act was of such frequent occurrence, so audaciously, so unblushingly public, that public morality demanded the strongest measures. That very night a descent was made upon the dwelling of the unconscious *Avocato.* The sanctity of the connubial chamber was invaded. The sleeping beauty of fifty was ordered to rise, and was dragged off to—the Convent of Repentant Females! B.......... knew, and none better, what manner of thing law was in Rome, so instead of wasting time in reasoning with the Pope as to the legality of the case—urging the argument that, even supposing his wife to have

The institution of the lottery is retained by the Popes, not as a source of revenue only. Lay governments have long since abolished it, because in a well-organized state, where industry leads to everything, citizens should be taught to rely upon nothing but their industry. But in the kingdom of the Church, where industry leads to nothing, not only is the lottery a consolation to the poor, but it forms an integral part of the public education. The sight of a beggar suddenly enriched, as it were by enchantment, goes far to make the ignorant multitude believe in miracles. The miracle of the loaves and fishes were scarcely more marvellous than the changing of tenpence into two hundred and fifty pounds. A high prize is like a present from God; it is money falling from Heaven. This people know that no human power can oblige three particular numbers to come out together; so they rely on the divine mercy alone. They apply to the Capuchin friars for lucky numbers; they recite special prayers for so many days; they humbly call for the inspiration of Heaven before going to bed; they see in dreams the Madonna stuck all over with figures; they pay for masses at the Churches; they offer the priest money if he will put three numbers under the chalice at the moment of the consecration. Not less humbly did the courtiers of Louis XIV. range themselves in the antechamber he was to pass through, in the hope of obtaining a look or a favour. The drawing of the lottery is public, as are the University

been of a susceptible age and an attractive exterior, so long as he himself made no objection to her driving out with the old Duke, nobody else had any right to interfere—and other similar appeals to common sense, he at once requested the interference of the French Ambassador. This was promptly and effectively given. The incarceration of the peccant dame was brief; and a shower of ridicule fell upon the Pontifical head. But the Sovereigns of Rome are accustomed to, and regardless of, such irreverent demonstrations.—TRANSL.

lectures in France. And, verily, it is a great and salutary lesson. The winners learn to praise God for his bounties: the losers are punished for having unduly coveted worldly pelf. Everybody profits—most of all the Government, which makes £80,000 a year by it, besides the satisfaction of having done its duty.

Yes, the holy preceptors of the nation fulfil their duty towards God, and towards themselves. But it does not necessarily follow that they always manage the affairs of God and of the Government well.

> "On rencontre sa destinée
> Souvent par les chemins qu'on prend pour l'éviter."

La Fontaine tells us this, and the Pope proves it to us. In spite of the attention paid to religious instruction, the sermons, the good books, the edifying spectacles, the lottery, and so many other good things, faith is departing. The general aspect of the country does not betray the fact, because the fear of scandal pervades all society; but the devil loses nothing by that. Perhaps the citizens have the greater dislike to religion, from the very fact of its reigning over them. Our master is our enemy. God is too much the master of these people not to be treated by them in some degree as an enemy.

The spirit of opposition is called atheism, where the Tuileries are called the Vatican. A young ragamuffin, who drove me from Rimini to Santa Maria, let slip a terrible expression, which I have often thought of since: "God?"—he said, "if there be one, I dare say he's a priest like the rest of 'em."

Reflect upon these words, reader! When I examine them closely, I start back in terror, as before those crevices of Vesuvius, which give you a glimpse of the abyss below.

Has the temporal power served its own interests better

than it has those of God ? I doubt it. The deputation of Rome was Red in 1848. It was Rome that chose Mazzini. It is Rome that still regrets him in the low haunts of the Regola, on that miry bank of the Tiber, where secret societies swarm at this moment, like gnats on the shores of the Nile.

If these deplorable fruits of a model education were pointed out to the philosopher Gavarni, he would probably exclaim, "Bring up nations, in order that they may hate and despise you!"

CHAPTER XVII.

FOREIGN OCCUPATION.

The Pope is loved and revered in all Catholic countries—except his own.

It is, therefore, perfectly just and natural that one hundred and thirty-nine millions of devoted and respectful men should render him assistance against three millions of discontented ones. It is not enough to have given him a temporal kingdom, or to have restored that kingdom to him when he had the misfortune to lose it; one must lend him a permanent support, unless the expense of a fresh restoration is to be incurred every year.

This is the principle of the foreign occupation. We are one hundred and thirty-nine millions of Catholics, who have violently delegated to three millions of Italians the honour of boarding and lodging our spiritual chief. If we were not to leave a respectable army in Italy to watch over the execution of our commands, we should be doing our work by halves.

In strict logic, the security of the Pope should be guaranteed at the common expense of the Catholic Powers. It seems quite natural that each nation interested in the oppression of the Romans should furnish its contingent of soldiers. Such a system, however, would have the effect of turning the castle of St. Angelo into another Tower of Babel. Besides, the affairs of this world are not all regulated according to the principles of logic.

The only three Powers which contributed to the re-establishment of Pius IX. were France, Austria, and Spain. The French besieged Rome; the Austrians seized the places of the Adriatic; the Spaniards did very little, not from the want either of goodwill or courage, but because their allies left them nothing to do.

If a private individual may be permitted to probe the motives upon which princes act, I would venture to suggest that the Queen of Spain had nothing in view but the interests of the Church. Her soldiers came to restore the Pope to his throne; they went as soon as he was reseated on it. This was a chivalrous policy.

Napoleon III. also considered the restoration of the Pope to a temporal throne necessary to the good of the Church. Perhaps he thinks so still—though I couldn't swear to it. But his motives of action were complicated. Simple President of the French Republic, heir to a name which summoned him to the throne, resolved to exchange his temporary magistracy for an imperial crown, he had the greatest possible interest in proving to Europe how republics are put down. He had already conceived the idea of playing that great part of champion of order, which has since caused him to be received by all Sovereigns first as a brother, and afterwards as an arbitrator. Lastly, he knew that the restoration of the Pope would secure him a million of Catholic votes towards his election to the imperial crown. But to these motives of personal interest were added some others, if possible, of a loftier character. The heir of Napoleon and of the liberal Revolution of '89, the man who read his own name on the first page of the civil code, the author of so many works breathing the spirit of new ideas and the passionate love of progress, the silent dreamer whose busy brain already teemed with the germs of all the prosperity we have enjoyed for the last ten years, was incapable of handing over three millions of Italians to reaction, lawlessness, and misery. If he had firmly resolved to put down the Republic at Rome, he was not less firm in his resolution to suppress the abuses, the injustice, and all the traditional oppressions which drove the Italians to revolt. In the opinion of the head of the French Republic, the way to be again victorious over anarchy, was to deprive it of all pretext and all cause for its existence.

He knew Rome; he had lived there. He knew, from personal experience, in what the Papal government differed from good governments. His natural sense of justice urged him to give the subjects of the Holy Father, in exchange for the political autonomy of which he robbed them, all the civil liberties and all the inoffensive rights enjoyed in civilized States.

On the 18th of August, 1849, he addressed to M. Edgar Ney a letter, which was, in point of fact, a *memorandum* addressed to the Pope. AMNESTY, SECULARIZATION, THE CODE NAPOLEON, A LIBERAL GOVERNMENT: these were the gifts he promised to the Romans in exchange for the Republic, and demanded of the Pope in return for a crown. This programme contained, in half-a-dozen words, a great lesson to the sovereign, and a great consolation to the people.

But it is easier to introduce a Breguet spring into a watch made when Henri IV. was king, than a single reform into the old pontifical machine. The letter of the 18th of August was received by the friends of the Pope as an "insult to his rights, good sense, justice, and majesty!" * Pius

* Louis Veuillot, article of the 10th of September, 1849.

IX. took offence at it; the Cardinals made a joke of it. This determination, this prudence, this justice, on the part of a man who held them all in his hand, appeared to them immeasurably comical. They still laugh at it. Don't name M. Edgar Ney before them, or you'll make them laugh till their sides ache.

The Emperor of Austria never committed the indiscretion of writing such a letter as that of the 18th of August. The fact is, the Austrian policy in Italy differs materially from ours.

France is a body very solid, very compact, very firm, very united, which has no fear of being encroached upon, and no desire to encroach on others. Her political frontiers are nearly her natural limits; she has little or nothing to conquer from her neighbours. She can, therefore, interfere in the events of Europe for purely moral interests, without views of conquest being attributed to her. One or two of her leaders have suffered themselves to be carried somewhat too far by the spirit of adventure; the nation has never had, what may be called, geographical ambition. France does not disdain to conquer the world by the dispersion of her ideas, but she desires nothing more. That which constitutes the beauty of our history, to those who take an elevated view of it, is the twofold object, pursued simultaneously by the Sovereign and the nation, of concentrating France, and spreading French ideas.

The old Austrian diplomacy has been, for the last six hundred years, incessantly occupied in stitching together bits of material, without ever having been able to make a coat. It does not consider either the colour or the quality of the cloth, but always keeps the needle going. The thread it uses is often white, and it not infrequently breaks—when away goes the new patch! Then another has to be found.

A province is detached—two more are laid hold of. The piece gets rent down the middle—a rag is caught up, then another, and whatever comes to hand is sewn together in breathless haste. The effect of this stitching monomania has been, to keep constantly changing the map of Europe, to bring together, as chance willed it, races and religions of every pattern, and to trouble the existence of twenty peoples, without making the unity of a nation. Certain Machiavellic old gentlemen sitting round a green cloth at Vienna, direct this work, measure the material, rub their hands complacently when it stretches, snatch off their wigs in despair when a piece is torn, and look on all sides for another wherewith to replace it. In the Middle Ages, the sons of the house used to be sent to visit foreign princesses: they made love to their royal and serene highnesses in German, and always brought back with them some shred of territory. But now that princesses receive their dowers in hard cash, recourse is had to violent measures in order to procure pieces of material; they are seized by soldiers; and there are some large stains of blood upon this harlequin's cloak!

Almost all the states of Italy, the kingdom of Naples, Sardinia, Sicily, Modena, Parma, Placentia, and Guastalla, have been in turn stitched to the same piece as Bohemia, Transylvania, and Croatia. Rome would have shared the same fate, if papal excommunications had not broken the thread. In 1859 it is Venice and Milan that pay for everybody, till it comes to the turn of Tuscany, Modena, and Massa, to be patched on in virtue of certain reversionary rights.

What must have been the satisfaction of Austrian diplomatists when they were enabled to throw their troops into the kingdom of the Pope, without remonstrances from anybody! Beyond all doubt, the interests of the Church were those which least occupied them. And as for taking any interest in the unfortunate subjects of Pius IX., or demanding for them any rights, or any liberties, Austria never thought of it for a moment. The old Danaïde only saw an opportunity for pouring another people into her ill-made and unretentive cask.

While the French army cautiously cannonaded the capital of the arts, spared public monuments, and took Rome, so to speak, with gloved hands, the Austrian soldiers carried the beautiful cities of the Adriatic—*à la Croate!* As victors, we treated gently those we had conquered, from motives of humanity; Austria, those she had conquered, brutally, from motives of conquest. She regarded the fair country of the Legations and the Marches as another Lombardy, which she would be well disposed to keep.

We occupied Rome, and the port of Civita Vecchia; the Austrians took for themselves all the country towards the Adriatic. We established our quarters in the barracks assigned to us by the municipality; the Austrians built complete fortresses, as is their practice, with the money of the people they were oppressing. For six or seven years their army lived at the expense of the country. They sent their regiments naked, and when poor Italy had clothed them, others came to replace them.

Their army was looked upon with no very favourable eye; neither indeed was ours: the radical party was opposed both to their presence and ours. Some stray soldiers of both armies were killed. The French army defended itself courteously, the Austrian army revenged itself. In three years, from the first of January, 1850, to the 1st of January, 1853, we shot three murderers. Austria has a heavier hand: she has executed not only criminals, but thoughtless, and even innocent people. I have already given some terrible figures, and will spare you their repetition.

From the day when the Pope condescended to return home, the French army withdrew into the background; it hastened to restore to the pontifical government all its powers. Austria has only restored what it could not keep. She even still undertakes to repress political crimes. She feels personally wronged if a cracker is let off, if a musket is concealed: in short, she fancies herself in Lombardy.

At Rome, the French place themselves at the disposal of the Pope for the maintenance of order and public security. Our soldiers have too much honesty to let a murderer or a thief who is within their reach escape. The Austrians pretend that they are not gendarmes, to arrest malefactors; each individual soldier considers himself the agent of the old diplomatists, charged with none but political functions: police matters are not within his province. What is the consequence? The Austrian army, after carefully disarming the citizens, delivers them over to malefactors, without the means of protection.

At Bologna, a merchant of the name of Vincenzio Bedini was pointed out to me, who had been robbed in his warehouse at six o'clock in the evening. An Austrian sentinel was on guard at his door.

Austria has good reasons for encouraging disorders in the provinces she occupies: the greater the frequency of crime, and the difficulty of governing the people, the greater is the necessity for the presence of an Austrian army. Every murder, every theft, every burglary, every assault, tends to strike the roots of these old diplomatists more deep into the kingdom of the Pope.

France would rejoice to be able to recall her troops. She feels that their presence at Rome is not a normal state of things: she is herself more shocked than anybody else at this irregularity. She has reduced, as much as possible, the effective force of her occupying army; she would embark her remaining regiments, were she not aware that to do so would be to deliver the Pope over to the executioner. Mark the extent to which she carries her disinterestedness in the affairs of Italy. In order to place the Holy Father in a condition to defend himself alone, she is trying to create for him a national army. The Pope possesses at the present time four regiments of French manufacture; if they are not very good, or rather, not to be relied upon, it is not the fault of the French. The priestly government has itself alone to blame. Our generals have done all in their power, not only to drill the Pope's soldiers, but to inspire them with that military spirit which the Cardinals carefully endeavour to stifle. Is it likely that we shall find the Austrian army seeking to render its presence needless, and spontaneously returning home?

And yet I must admit, with a certain shame, that the conduct of the Austrians is more logical than ours. They entered the Pope's dominions, meaning to stay there; they spare no pains to assure their conquest in them. They decimate the population, in order that they may be feared. They perpetuate disorder, in order that their permanent presence may be required. Disorder and terror are Austria's best arms.

As for us, let us see what we have done. In the interest of France, nothing; and I am glad of it. In the interest of the Pope, very little. In the interest of the Italian nation, still less.

The Pope promised us the reform of some abuses, in his *Motu Proprio* of Portici. It was not quite what we demanded of him; still his promises afforded us some gratification He returned to his capital, to elude their fulfilment at his ease. Our soldiers awaited him with arms in their hands. They fell at his feet as he passed them.

During nine consecutive years, the pontifical government has been retreating step by step,—France, all the while, politely entreating it to move on a little. Why should it follow our advice? What necessity was there for yielding to our arguments? Our soldiers continued to mount guard, to present arms, to fall down on one knee, and patrol regularly round all the old abuses.

In the end, the pertinacity with which we urged our good counsels became disagreeable to his Holiness. His retrograde court has a horror of us; it prefers the Austrians, who crush the people, but who never talk of liberty. The Cardinals say, sometimes in a whisper, sometimes even aloud, that they don't want our army, that we are very much in their way, and that they could protect themselves—with the assistance of a few Austrian regiments.

The nation, that is the middle class, says, our good-will, of which it has no doubt, is of little use to it; and declares it would undertake to obtain all its rights, to secularize the government, to proclaim the amnesty, to introduce the Code Napoléon, and to establish liberal institutions, if we would but withdraw our soldiers. This is what it says at Rome. At Bologna, Ferrara, and Ancona, it believes that, in spite of everything, the Romans are glad to have us, because, although we let evil be done, we never do it ourselves. In this we are admitted to be better than the Austrians.

Our soldiers say nothing. Troops don't argue under arms. Let me speak for them.

" We are not here to support the injustice and dishonesty of a petty government that would not be tolerated for twenty-four hours with us. If we were, we must change the eagle on our flags for a crow. The Emperor cannot desire the misery of a people, and the shame of his soldiers. He has his own notions. But if, in the meantime, these poor devils of Romans were to rise in insurrection, in the hope of obtaining the Secularization, the Amnesty, the Code, and the Liberal Government, which we have taught them to expect, we should inevitably be obliged to shoot them down."

CHAPTER XVIII.

WHY THE POPE WILL NEVER HAVE SOLDIERS.

I PAID a visit to a Roman Prelate well known for his devotion to the interests of the Church, the temporal power of the Popes, and the august person of the Holy Father.

When I was introduced to his oratory I found him reading over the proof-sheets of a thick volume, entitled ADMINISTRATION OF THE MILITARY FORCES.

He threw down his pen with an air of discouragement, and showed me the two following quotations which he had inscribed on the title-page of the book:

"Every independent State should suffice to itself, and assure its internal security by its own forces."—*Count de Rayneval, note of 14th May*, 1855.

"The troops of the Pope will always be the troops of the Pope. What are warriors who have never made war?"—*De Brosses.*

After I had reflected a little upon these not very consoling passages, the Prelate said, "You have not been very long at Rome, and your impressions ought to be just, because they are fresh. What do you think of our Romans? Do the descendants of Marius appear to you a race without courage, incapable of confronting danger? If it be indeed true that the nation has retained nothing of its patrimony, not even its physical courage, all our efforts to create a national force in Rome are foredoomed to failure. The Popes must for ever remain disarmed in the presence of their enemies. Nothing is left for them but to entrench themselves behind the mercenary courage of a Swiss garrison or the respectful protection of a great Catholic power. What becomes of independence? What becomes of sovereignty?"

"Monsignore," I replied, "I already know the Romans too well to judge them by the calumnies of their enemies. I daily see with what intemperate courage this violent and hot-blooded people gives and receives death. I know the esteem expressed by Napoleon I. for the regiments he raised here. And we can say between ourselves that there were many of the subjects of the Pope in the revolutionary army which defended Rome against the French. I am persuaded, then, that the Holy Father has no need to go abroad to find men, and that a few years would serve to make these men good soldiers. What is much less evident to me is the real necessity for having a Roman army. Does the Pope want to aggrandise himself by war? No. Does he fear lest some enemy should invade his States? Certainly not. He is better protected by the veneration of Europe than by a line of fortresses. If, by a scarcely possible eventuality, any difference were to arise between the Holy See and an Italian Monarchy, the Pope has the means of resistance at hand, without striking a blow; for he counts more soldiers in Piedmont, in Tuscany, and in the Two Sicilies, than the Neapolitans, the Tuscans, and the Piedmontese would well know how to send against him. So much for the exterior; and the situation is so clear, that your Ministry of War assumes the modest and Christian title of 'the Ministry of Arms.' As for the interior, a good gendarmerie is all you want.'

" Eh! my dear son," cried the Prelate, " we ask nothing better. A people which is never destined to make war does not want an army, but it ought to keep on foot the forces necessary for the maintenance of the public peace. An army of police and internal security is what we have been endeavouring to create since 1849. Have we succeeded? Do we suffice for ourselves? Are we in a position to ensure our tranquillity by our own forces? No! no! certainly not."

" Pardon me, Monsignore, if I think you a little severe. During the three months I have loitered as an observer in Rome, I have had time to see the pontifical army. Your soldiers are fine-looking men, their general appearance is good, they have a martial air, and, as far as I can judge, they go through their manœuvres pretty well. It would be difficult to recognize in them the old soldier of the Pope, the fabulous personage whose duty it was to escort processions, and to fire off the cannon on firework nights; the well-to-do citizen in uniform who, if the weather looked threatening, mounted guard with an umbrella. The Holy Father's army would present a good appearance in any country in the world; and there are some of your soldiers whom—at a little distance—I should take for our own."

" Yes," he said, " their appearance is good enough, and if factions could be kept down by mere appearances, I should feel tolerably easy. But I know many things respecting the army that make me very uncomfortable—and yet I don't know all. I know there is great difficulty in recruiting not only soldiers, but officers; that young men of good family scorn to command, and ploughboys to serve, in our army. I know that more than one mother would rather see her son at the hulks than with the regiment. I know that our soldiers, for the most part drawn from the dregs of the people, have neither confidence in their comrades, nor respect for their officers, nor veneration for their colours. You would vainly look to find among them devotion to their country, fidelity to their sovereign, and all those high and soldierly virtues which make a man die at his post. To the greater number the laws of duty and honour are a dead letter. I know that the gendarme does not always respect private property. I know that the factions rely at least much as we ourselves do on the support of the army. What good is it to us to have fourteen or fifteen thousand men on foot, and to spend some millions of scudi annually, if after such efforts and sacrifices, foreign protection is now more necessary to us than it was the first day ?"

"Monsignore," I replied, "you place things in the worst light, and you judge the situation somewhat after the manner of the Prophet Jeremiah. The Holy Father has several excellent officers, both in the special corps and in the regiments of the line; and you have also some good soldiers. Our officers, who are competent men, render justice to yours, both as regards their intelligence and their goodwill. If I am astonished at anything, it is that the pontifical army has made so much progress as it has in the deplorable conditions in which it is placed. We can discuss it freely because the whole system is under examination, and about to be reorganized by the Head of the State. You complain that young gentlemen of good family do not throng to the College of Cadets in the hope of gaining an epaulette. But you forget how little the epaulette is honoured among you. The officer has no rank in the state. It is a settled point that a deacon shall have precedence of a sub-deacon; but the law and custom of Rome do not allow a Colonel to take precedence even of a man having the simple tonsure. Pray, what position do you assign to your Generals? What is their rank in the hierarchy?"

"Instead of having our Generals in the army, we have them at the head of the religious orders. Imagine the sensations of the General of the Jesuits at hearing a soldier announced by the honourable ecclesiastical title of GENERAL!"

"Well! there's something in that."

"In order to have commanders for our troops, without at the same time creating personages of too much importance, we have imported three foreign Colonels, who are permitted to perform the functions of General. They even appear in the disguise of Generals, but they will never have the audacity to assume the title."

"Capital! Well, now with us there is not a scamp of eighteen who would engage in the army if he were told that he might become a Colonel, but never a General; or even a General, but never a Marshal of France. Who, or what, could induce a man to rush into a career in which there is at a certain point an impassable barrier? You regret that all your officers are not *savants*. I admit that they have learnt something. They enter the College without competition or preliminary examination, sometimes without orthography or arithmetic. The first inspection made by our Generals discovers future lieutenants who cannot do a sum in division, a French class without either a master or pupils, and an historical class in which, after seven months of teaching, the professor is still theologically expounding the creation of the world. It must indeed be a powerful spirit of emulation which can induce these young men to make themselves capable of keeping up a conversation with French officers. You are astonished that they allow the discipline of their men to become somewhat relaxed. Why, discipline is about the last thing they have been taught. In the time of Gregory XVI. an officer refused to allow a Cardinal's carriage to pass down a certain street. Such were his orders. The coachman drove on, and the officer was sent to the castle of St. Angelo, for having done his duty. A single instance of this sort is quite enough to demoralize an army. But the King of Naples shows the Pope his mistake. He had a sentry mentioned in the order of the day, for giving a bishop's coachman a cut with his sword. You are scandalized because certain military administrators curtail the soldiers' poor allowance of bread; but they have never been told that peculation will be punished by dismissal."

"Well, the scheme of reorganization is in hand; you will see a new order of things in 1859."

"I am glad to hear it, Monsignore; and I will answer for it that a judicious, well-considered reform—slowly progressive, of course, as everything is at Rome—will produce excellent results in a few years. It is not in a day that you can expect to change the face of things; but you know the gardener is not discouraged by the certainty that the tree he plants to-day will not produce fruit for the next five years. The morals of your soldiers are, as you say, none of the best: I hear it said everywhere that an honest peasant thinks it a dishonour to wear your uniform. When you can hold out a future to your men, you need no longer recruit them from the dregs of the population. The soldier will have some feeling of personal dignity when he ceases to find himself exposed to contempt. These poor fellows are looked down upon by everybody, even by the servants of small families. They breathe an atmosphere of scorn, which may be termed the *malaria* of honour. Relieve them, Monsignore; they ask nothing better."

"Do you think, then, the means are to be found of giving us an army as proud and as faithful as the French army?

That were a secret for which the Cardinal would pay a high price."

"I offer it to you for nothing, Monsignore. France has always been the most military country in Europe; but in the last century the French soldier was no better than yours. The officers are pretty much the same, with this difference only,—that formerly the King selected them from the nobility, whereas now they ennoble themselves by zeal and courage. But a hundred years ago the soldiery, properly so called, consisted in France of what it now does with you—the scum of the population. Picked up in low taverns, between a heap of crown-pieces and a glass of brandy, the soldier made himself more dreaded by the peasantry than by the enemy. He seemed to be overpowered beneath the weight of the scorn of the country at large, the meanness of his present condition, and the impossibility of future promotion; and he revenged himself by forays upon the cellar and the farmyard. He had his place among the scourges which desolated monarchical France. Hear what La Fontaine says,—

> "La faim, les créanciers, *les soldats*, la corvée,
> Lui font d'un malheureux la peinture achevée."

You see that your soldiers of 1858 are angels in comparison with our *soudards* of the monarchy. If, with all this, you still find them not absolutely perfect, try the French recipe: submit all your citizens to a conscription, in order that your regiments may not be composed of the refuse of the nation. Create—"

"Stop!" cried the prelate.

"Monsignore?"

"I stopped you short, my son, because I perceive that you are getting beyond the real and the possible. *Primo*, we have no citizens; we have subjects. *Secundo*, the conscription is a revolutionary measure, which we will not adopt at any price; it consecrates a principle of equality as much opposed to the ideas of the Government as to the habits of the country. It might possibly give us a very good army, but that army would belong to the nation, not to the Sovereign. We will at once put away, if you please, this dangerous utopia."

"It might gain you some popularity."

"Far from it. Believe me, the subjects of the Holy Father have a deep antipathy to the principle of the conscription. The discontent of La Vendée and Brittany is nothing to that which it would create here."

"People become accustomed to everything, Monsignore. I have met contingents from La Vendée and Brittany singing merrily as they went to join their corps."

"So much the better for them. But let me tell you the only grievance of this country against the French rule is the conscription, which the Emperor had established among us."

"So you negative my proposal of the conscription."

"Absolutely!"

"I must think no more about it?"

"Quite out of the question."

"Well, Monsignore, I'll do without it. Let us have recourse to the system of voluntary enlistment, but with the condition that you secure the prospects of the soldier. What bounty do you offer to recruits?"

"Twelve scudi; but for the future we mean to go as high as twenty."

"Twenty scudi is fair enough; still I'm afraid even at one hundred and seven francs a head you won't get picked men. Now, you will allow, Monsignore, a peasant must be badly off indeed when a bounty of twenty scudi tempts him to put on a uniform which is universally despised? But if you want to attract more recruits round every barrack than there were suitors at Penelope's gate, endow the army, offer the Roman citizens—pardon me, I mean the Pope's *subjects* —such a bounty as is really likely to tempt them. Pay them down a small sum for the assistance of their families, and keep the balance till their period of service has expired. Induce them to re-engage after their discharge by promises honourably and faithfully observed; arrange that with every additional year of service the savings which the soldier has left in the hands of the state shall increase. Believe me, when the Romans know that a soldier, without assistance, without education, without any brilliant action, or any stroke of good fortune, by the mere faithful performance of his duty, can, after twenty-five years' service, secure an income of £20 or £25 a year, they will snatch at the advantage of entering the ranks; and I warrant you, the personal interest of each will attach them more firmly to the Government, as the depository of their savings. When the house of a notary is on fire you will see the most immovable and indifferent of shopkeepers running like a cat on the tiles, to put out the fire and save his own papers. On the same principle, a Government will always be served with zeal in proportion to the interest its servants have in its security."

"Of course," said the Prelate, "I understand your argument perfectly. Man requires some object in life. A hundred and twenty scudi a year is not an unpleasant bed to lie upon after a term of military service. At this price we should not want candidates. Even the middle class would solicit employment in the military as much as it now does the civil service of the state; and we should be able to pick and choose our men. What frightens me in the matter is the expense."

"Ah! Monsignore, you know a really good article is

never to be had cheap. The Pontifical Government has 15,000 soldiers for £400,000. France would pay half as much again for them: but then she would have the value of the extra cost. The men who have completed three or four terms of service, are those who cost the most money; and yet there is an economy in keeping them, because every such man is worth three conscripts. Do you then, or do you not, wish to create a national force? Have you made up your mind on the subject? If you do wish for it, you must pay for it, and make the sacrifices necessary to obtain it. If, on the contrary, your Government prefers economy to security, begin by saving the £400,000, and sell to some foreign country the 15,000 muskets, more dangerous than useful, since you don't know whether they are for you or against you. The question may be summed up in two words: safety, which will cost you money; or economy, which may cost you your existence!"

"You are proposing an army of Prætorians."

"The name is not the thing. I only promise you that if you pay your soldiers well, they'll be faithful to you."

"The Prætorians often turned against the Emperors."

"Because the Emperors were silly enough to pay them ready money."

"But is there no motive in this world nobler than interest? And is money the only lasting tie that binds soldiers to their standard?"

"I should not be a Frenchman, if I held such a belief. I advised you to increase your soldiers' pay, because hitherto your army has been recruited by money alone; and also because money is that which it costs you the least to obtain, and consequently that which you will the most willingly part with. Well then, now that you have given me the few millions I required for the purpose of attaching your soldiers to the Pontifical Government, furnish me with the means of raising them in their own estimation and in that of the people. Honour them, in order that they may become men of honour. Prove to them, by the consideration with which you surround them, that they are not footmen, and that they ought not to have the souls of footmen. Give them a place in the state; throw around their uniform some of the *prestige* which is now the exclusive privilege of the clerical garb."

"Do you know what you are asking for?"

"Nothing but what is absolutely necessary. Remember, Monsignore, that this army, raised to act in the interior of the Pontifical States, will serve you less frequently by the force of its arms, than by the moral authority of its presence. And pray what authority can it possess in the eyes of your subjects, if the Government affect to despise it?"

"But, admitting that it obtain all the pay and all the consideration that you claim for it, still it will remain open to the remark of the President de Brosses, 'What are warriors who have never in their lives made war?'"

"I admit it. The consideration accorded by all Frenchmen to the soldier, takes its source in the idea of the dangers he has encountered or may encounter. We behold in him a man who has sacrificed his life beforehand, in engaging to shed every drop of his blood at a word from his chiefs. If the little children in our country respectfully salute the colours—that steeple of the regiment—it is because they think on the brave fellows who have fallen round it."

"Perhaps, then, you think we ought to send our soldiers to make war, before employing them as guardians of the peace?"

"It is certain, Monsignore, that whenever one sees an old Crimean soldier who has strayed into one of the Pope's foreign regiments, the medal he wears on his breast makes him look quite a different man from any of his comrades. The corps of your army which the people has treated with the greatest respect, is the Pontifical Carabineers, because it was originally formed of Napoleon's old soldiers."

"My friend, you do not answer my question. Do you require us to declare war against Europe for the sake of teaching our gendarmes to keep the peace at home?"

"Monsignore, the government of his Holiness is too prudent to go in search of adventures. We are no longer in the days of Julius II., who donned the cuirass, and buckled on the sword of the flesh, and sprang himself into the breach. But why should not the Head of the Church do as Pius V., who sent his sailors with the Spaniards and Venetians to the battle of Lepanto? Why should you not detach a regiment or two to Algeria? France would, perhaps, give them a place in her army; they might join us in advancing the holy cause of civilization. Rest assured that when those troops returned, after five or six campaigns, to the more modest duty of preserving the public peace, everybody would obey them courteously. Vulgar footmen would no longer dare to make use of such expressions as one I heard yesterday evening at the door of a theatre,—'Stick to your soldiering, and leave servant's work to me!' They who despise them now, would be proud to show them respect; for nations have a tendency to admire themselves in the persons of their armies."

"For how long?"

"For ever. Acquired glory is a capital which can never be exhausted. And these regiments would never lose the spirit of honour and discipline which they would bring back from the seat of war. You know not, Monsignore, what it is to have an idea become incarnate in a regiment. There is a whole world of recollections, traditions, and virtues, circulating, seen and unseen, through this band of men. It is the moral patrimony of the corps; the veterans don't carry it away when they retire from the service, while the conscripts inherit it from the day of their joining the regiment. The colonel, the officers, and the privates, change one after the other, and yet it is the same regiment that ever remains, because the same spirit continues to flutter amid the folds of the same colours. Have four good regiments of picked men, well paid, properly respected, and that have been under fire, and they will last as long as Rome, and Mazzini himself will not prevail against their courage."

"So be it! And may Heaven hear you!"

"The business is half done, Monsignore, when you have heard me. We are not far from the Vatican, where sits the real Minister of Arms."

"He will urge another objection."

"What will it be?"

"That if he send our regiments to serve their appren ticeship in Africa, they will bring back French ideas."

"That is an accident, impossible to prevent. But console yourself with the reflection that it is perfectly immaterial whether the French ideas are brought into your country by your soldiers or by ours. Besides, this is an article which so easily eludes the vigilance of the custom-house, that the railways are already bringing it in daily, and you will soon have a large stock on hand. And after all, where's the great evil? All men who have studied us without prejudice, know that French ideas are ideas of order and liberty, of conservatism and progress, of labour and honesty, of culture and industry. The country in which French ideas abound the most is France, and France, Monsignore, is in good health."

CHAPTER XIX.

MATERIAL INTERESTS.

"For my part," said a great fat Neapolitan, "I don't care the value of a bit of orange-peel for politics. I am willing to believe we've got a bad government, because all the world says we have, and because our King never dare show himself in public. All I can say is, that my grandfather made 20,000 ducats as a manufacturer; that my father doubled his capital in trade; and that I bought an estate which, in my tenants' hands, pays me six per cent. for the investment. I eat four meals a day, I'm in vigorous health, and I weigh fourteen stone. So when I toss off my third glass of old Capri wine at supper, I can't for the life of me help crying, 'Long live the King!'"

A huge hog which happened to cross the street as the Neapolitan reached his climax, gave a grunt in token of approbation.

The "hog" school is not numerous in Italy, whatever superficial travellers may have told you on that head. The most highly-gifted nation in Europe will not easily be persuaded that the great end of human existence is to eat four meals a day.

But let us suppose for an instant that all the Pope's subjects are willing to renounce all liberty,—religious, political, municipal, and even civil,—for the sake of growing sleek and fat, without any higher aim, and are content with the merely animal enjoyments of health and food; do they find in their homes the means of satisfying their wants? Can they, on that score at least, applaud their Government? Are they as well treated as beasts in a cage? Are the people fat and thriving? I answer, No!

In every country in the world the sources of public wealth are three in number: agriculture, manufactures, and commerce. All governments which do their duty, and understand their interests, emulate one another in favouring, by wholesome administrative measures, the farm, the workshop, and the counting-house. Wherever the nation and its rulers are united, trade and manufactures will be found clinging round the government, and increasing even to excess the population of the capital cities; while agriculture works her greatest miracles in the circuit which is the most immediately subject to the influence of authority.

Rome is the least industrious and commercial city in the Pontifical States, and its suburbs resemble a desert. You must travel very far to find any industrial experiment, or any attempt at trade.

Whose fault is this? Industrial pursuits require, above all things, liberty. Now in the States of the Church all the manufactures of any importance constitute privileges bestowed by the government upon its friends. Not only tobacco and salt, but sugar, glass, wax, and stearine, are objects of privilege. Privilege here — privilege there — privilege everywhere. An Insurance Company is established, of course by special privilege. The very baskets used by the cherry-vendors are the monopoly of a privileged basket-maker. The Inspector of the Piazza Navona* would seize

* The principal market in Rome is held in this Piazza.

any refractory basket which had failed to pay its tribute to monopoly. The grocers of Tivoli, the butchers of Frascati, all the retail dealers in the suburbs of Rome, are privileged. The system of privileges and monopolies is universal, and of course commerce shares the common lot.

Commerce cannot flourish without capital, facilities of credit, easy communication, and, above all, personal safety. I have shown you what the roads are as to safety. I have not yet shown you how wretchedly bad and insufficient they are. Now for a few facts.

In June, 1858, I travelled through the Mediterranean provinces, taking notes as I went along. I established the fact that in one township the bread cost nearly three-halfpence a pound, while in another, some twelve miles off, it was to be had for a penny. It follows that the carriage of goods along twelve miles of road cost a farthing a pound. At Sonnino bad wine was sold for sevenpence the *litre*, while the same quantity of passable wine might be had at Pagliano, thirty miles off, for twopence halfpenny; so the cost of carrying an article weighing some two pounds for thirty miles was fourpence halfpenny. Wherever governments make roads, prices naturally find their level.

I may be told that I explored remote and out-of-the-way districts. If we approach the capital, we find the matters still worse. The nearest villages to Rome have not roads fit for carriages from one to the other. What would be said of the French administration, if people could not get from Versailles to St. Germain without passing through Paris? This, however, has been for centuries the state of things near the Pope's capital. If you want a still more striking instance, here it is. Bologna, the second city in the Pontifical States, is in rapid and frequent communication with the whole world—except Rome. It despatches seven mails a week to foreign countries—only five to Rome. The letters from Paris arrive at Bologna some hours before those from Rome; the letters from Vienna are in advance of those from Rome by a day and a night. The Papal kingdom is not very extensive, but it seems to me even too extensive, when I see distances trebled by the carelessness of the Government and the inadequacy of the public works. As to railways, there are two, one from Rome to Frascati, and one from Rome to Civita Vecchia; but the Adriatic provinces, which are the most populous, the most energetic, and the most interesting in the country, will not hear the whistle of the locomotive and the rush of the train for a long time to come. The nation loudly demands railways. The lay proprietors, instead of absurdly asking fancy prices for their land, eagerly offer it to companies. The convents alone raise barricades, as if they thought the devil was trying to break in at their gates. The erection of a railway station in Rome gave rise to some comical difficulties. Our unfortunate engineers were utterly at a loss for the means of effecting an opening. On all sides the way was blocked up by obstructive friars. Black friars—white friars—grey friars—and brown friars. They began with the Lazarists. The Holy Father personally came to their rescue. "Ah, Mr. Engineer, have mercy on my poor Lazarists! The good souls are given to prayer and meditation; and your locomotives do make such a hideous din!" So Mr. Engineer is fain to try the neighbouring convent. New difficulties there. The next attack is made upon a little nunnery founded by the Princess de Bauffremont. But I have neither time nor space for episodical details. It suffices for our purpose to state that the construction of railways will be a terribly long-winded affair, and that in the meantime trade languishes for want of cross-roads. The budget of public works is devoted to the repair of churches, and the building of basilicas. Nearly half-a-million sterling has already been sunk in the erection of a very grey and very ugly edifice on the Ostia road.* As much more will be required to finish it, and the commerce of the country will be none the better.

Half a million sterling! Why the entire capital of the bank of Rome is but £400,000; and when merchants go there to have their bills discounted, they can get no money. They are obliged to apply to usurers and monopolists, and the governor of the bank is one. Rome has an Exchange. I discovered its existence by mere chance, in turning over a Roman almanack. This public establishment opens *once a week,* a fact which gives some idea of the amount of business transacted there.

If trade and manufactures offer but small resources to the subjects of his Holiness, they fortunately find some compensation in agriculture. The natural fertility of the soil, and the stubborn industry of those who cultivate it, will always suffice to keep the nation from starvation. While it pays away a million sterling annually for foreign manufactures, the surplus of its agricultural produce brings back some £800,000. Hemp and corn, oil and wool, wine, silk, and cattle, form its substantial wealth.

How do we find the Government acting in this respect? Its duties are very simple, and may be summed up in three words,—protection, assistance, and encouragement.

The budget is not heavily burdened under the head of encouragement. Some proprietors and land stewards, residing in Rome, ask permission to found an Agricultural Society. The authorities refuse. In order to attain their object, they steal furtively into a Horticultural Society, already estab-

* The Basilica of St. Paul without the walls.

lished by authority. They organize themselves, raise sub scriptions, exhibit to the Romans a good collection of cattle and distribute some gold and silver medals offered by Prince Cesarini. Is it not curious that an exhibition of cattle, in order to be tolerated, is obliged to smuggle itself in under the shelter of camellias and geraniums?

Lay sovereigns not only openly favour agriculture, but they encourage it at a heavy cost, and do not consider their money thrown away. They are well aware that to give a couple of hundred pounds to the inventor of a good plough, is to place a small capital out at a heavy interest. The investment will render their kingdom more prosperous, and their children more wealthy. But the Pope has no children. He prefers sowing in his churches, in order to reap the harvest in Paradise.

Might he not at least assist the unfortunate peasants who furnish the bread he eats?

An able and truthful statistician (the Marchese Pepoli) has proved that in the township of Bologna, the rural proprietors actually pay taxes to the amount of £6. 8*s.* 4*d.* upon every £4-worth of taxable income. The fisc is not content with absorbing the entire revenue, but it annually eats into the capital. What think you of such moderation?

In 1855 the vines were diseased everywhere. Lay governments vied with each other in assisting the distressed proprietors. Cardinal Antonelli seized the opportunity to impose a tax of £74,680 upon the vines; and as there were no grapes that year to pay it, the amount was charged upon the different townships. Now which has proved the heaviest scourge—the *Oidium* or the Cardinal Minister? Certainly not the *Oidium*, for that has disappeared. The Cardinal remains.

All the corn harvested in the *Agro Romano* pays a fixed

duty of twenty-two pauls per rubbio. The rubbio is worth, on an average, from 80 to 100 pauls; so that the government taxes the harvest to the amount of at least 22 per cent. Here is a moderate tax. Why it is more than double the tithe. So much for the assistance rendered to the growers of corn.

Every description of agricultural produce pays a tax on export. There are governments which give a premium to exporters: one may call that encouraging the national industry. There are others, and they are still more numerous, which allow a free export of the surplus produce of the land: this is not merely to encourage, it is to assist the labourers. The Pope levies an average tax of 22 per thousand on the total amount of exports, 160 per thousand on the value of imports. The Piedmontese government is satisfied with 13 per thousand on exports, and 58 per thousand on imports. Of the two countries, I should prefer farming in Piedmont.

Cattle are subject to vexatious taxes, which add from twenty to thirty per cent. to their cost. They pay when at pasture; they pay nearly twenty-three shillings per head at market; they pay on exportation. And yet the breeding of cattle is one of the most valuable resources of the State, and one of those which ought to be the most assisted.

The horses raised in the country pay five per cent. on their value every time they change hands. By the time a horse has passed through twenty different hands, the Government has pocketed as much as the breeder. When I say the Government, I am wrong; the horse-tax is not included in the Budget. It is an ecclesiastical prebend. Cardinal della Dateria throws it in with general episcopal revenues.

"The good shepherd should shear, and not flay his sheep." These are the words of an Emperor, not a Pope, of Rome.

And now I dare not ask of the Holy Father certain protective measures which could not fail to double the revenue of his crown and the number of his subjects.

According to the statistical returns of 1857, the territorial wealth of the Romans is estimated at £104,400,000. The gross produce of this capital does not reach more than £116,563. 11*s.* 8*d.*, or about ten per cent. This is little. In Poland, and some other great agricultural countries, the land pays a net revenue of twelve per cent., which represents at least twenty per cent. gross. The Roman soil would produce the same if the Roman government did its duty.

The country is divided into cultivated and uncultivated lands. The former, that is to say those planted with useful trees, enriched by manure, regularly submitted to manual labour, and sown every year, lie chiefly in the provinces of the Adriatic, far beyond the ken of the Pope. In this half of the States of the Church (the most worthy of attention, and the least known) twenty years of French occupation have left excellent traditions. The system of primogeniture is abolished, if not by law, at least in practice. The equality of rights among the children of the same father necessitates the subdivision of property so favourable to agricultural progress. There are some large landed proprietors here, as there are everywhere; but instead of abandoning their estates to the rapacity of an intendant, they divide them into different occupations, which they confide to the best farmers. The landlord supplies the land, the buildings, and the cattle, and pays the property-tax. The tenant supplies the labour, and pays the other taxes, and the produce is equally shared between the landlord and the tenant. The system answers well, and the Adriatic provinces would hardly seem deserving of pity, if it were not for the brigands, the inundations of the Po and the Reno, and the crushing taxation I have described.

These taxes are lighter on the other side of the Apennines. There are even in the neighbourhood of Rome some landowners who pay scarcely any at all. In 1854 the *Consulta di Stato* valued the privileged lands at £360,000. But we will turn to the subject of the uncultivated lands.

Towards the Mediterranean, north, east, south, and west of Rome, and wherever the Papal benediction extends, the flat country, which covers an immense extent, is at once uninhabited, uncultivated, and unhealthy. Various are the modes in which experienced persons have attempted to account for the wretched condition of this fine country.

One says, "It is uncultivated because it is uninhabited. How can you cultivate without men? It is uninhabited because it is unwholesome. How can you expect men to inhabit it at the risk of their lives? Make it healthy, and it will populate itself, and the population will cultivate it, for there is not a finer soil in the world."

Another replies, "You are wrong. You confound cause with effect. The country is unhealthy because it is uncultivated. The decayed vegetable matter accumulated by centuries ferments under the summer sun. The wind blows over it, and raises up a provision of subtle miasma, imperceptible to the smell, and yet destructive to life. If all these plains were ploughed or dug up three or four times, so as to let the air and light penetrate into the depths of the soil, the fever which lies dormant under the rank vegetation would speedily evaporate, and return no more. Hasten then to bring ploughs, and your first crop will be one of health."

A third replies to the two first, "You are both right. The country is unhealthy because it is uncultivated, and uncultivated because it is unhealthy. The question lies in a vicious circle, from which there is no escape. Let us therefore leave things as they are; and when the fever-season arrives, we can go and inhale the fresh mountain air under the tall trees of Frascati."

The last speaker, if I am not greatly mistaken, is a Prelate. But have a care, Monsignore! Frascati, once so renowned for the purity of its air, now no longer deserves its reputation; and I may say the same of Tivoli. The quarters of Rome most remarkable for healthiness, such for instance as the Pincian, have of late become unhealthy. Fever is gaining ground. It is equally worthy of observation that at the same time the cultivation of the land is diminishing; and that the estates in mortmain—that is to say, delivered into the hands of the priesthood—have been increasing at the yearly rate of from £60,000 to £80,000 a year. Is *mortmain* indeed the hand which kills?

I submitted this delicate question to a very intelligent, very honourable, and very wealthy man, who farms several thousand acres of Church property. He is one of the *Mercanti di Campagna*, mentioned in a former chapter (Chap. VI.). The following is the substance of his reply.

"Six-tenths of the Agro Romano are held in mortmain. Three-tenths belong to the princely families, and the remaining tenth to different individuals.

"I hold under a religious community. I have a three-years' lease of the bare land. The live and dead farm-stock is my own property. It represents an enormous capital, which is liable to all sorts of accidents. But in our dear country one must risk a great deal to gain a little.

"If the land, which is almost all of fine quality, were my own, I should bring nearly the whole of it under the plough; but I am expressly forbidden by a clause in my lease to break up the best land, for fear of exhausting it by growing corn. No doubt such would be the result in the course of time, because we apply no manure; but of course the inferior land which I *am* allowed to break up will be worn out much sooner, and will in the end become almost worthless. The monks knowing this, take care that the best land shall not lose its quality, and oblige me to keep it in pasture for cattle. Thus I grow little corn merely because the good fathers will not let me grow a great deal. I cultivate first one piece of land, then another. On my farm, as throughout the Agro Romano, cultivation is but a passing accident; and so long as this continues, the country will be unhealthy.

"I raise cattle, which, as you will presently see, is sometimes a profitable pursuit, sometimes quite the contrary. On the whole of my farm I have no shelter for my cattle. I asked the monks to build me some sheds, offering to pay an increased rent in proportion to outlay. The monk who acts as the man of business of the convent, shrugged his shoulders. 'What can you be thinking of?' he said; 'you know we have only a life interest in the property. To comply with your request, we must spend our income for the benefit of our successors: and what care we for our successors? No, we look to the present usufruct; the future is no concern of ours—we have no children!' And the friar is right. Well, he went on to say that I was at liberty to build at my own cost as many sheds as I liked, which of course would belong to the convent at the expiration of my lease. I replied that I had no objection to erect the sheds, if the convent would grant me a lease of reasonable length. But just then it occurred to me very opportunely, that the canon law does not recognize leases for more than three years, and that on the very day when my sheds were completed, the pious fathers might find it convenient to pick a quarrel with me. So here the matter dropped. Although our cattle are naturally hardy they are bound to suffer from exposure to the weather. A hundred cows under shelter will yield the same quantity of milk through the winter as five hundred in the open air, at half the cost. A large portion of the hay we strew about the pastures for the cattle, is trodden underfoot and spoilt instead of being eaten; and if rain falls, the whole is spoilt. Calculate the loss of milk, the cost of cartage over a wide range of land, the damage done to the pastures by the trampling of heavy cattle in wet weather, all caused by the want of a few sheds, which it is impossible to have under the present system, and you will appreciate the position of a farmer holding under landlords who are careless as to the future, and merely live from hand to mouth.

"There is another improvement, which I offered to make at my own expense. I asked permission to dam up a little stream, dig some trenches, and irrigate the fields, by which I could have doubled the produce both in quantity and quality. You will hardly imagine the answer I received. The monks declared the extraordinary fertility which would result from the irrigation, would be a sort of violence done to nature, by which in the end the soil could not fail to be impoverished. What could I reply to such reasoning? These good fathers only think of nursing their income. I tax them neither with ignorance nor bad intentions. I only regret that the land should be in their hands.

"Pasture-farming under such conditions as these is a terribly hazardous pursuit. A single year of drought will suffice to ruin a breeder completely. In the years 1854–5 we lost from twenty to forty per cent. of our cattle; in 1856–7 from seventeen to twenty per cent.: and bear in mind that every beast, before it died, had been taxed."

A champion of the Pontifical system offered to prove to

me *by figures* that all is for the best even in the ecclesiastical estates.

"We have our reasons," he said, "for preferring pasture to arable land. Here is a property consisting of a hundred *rubbia** (not quite three hundred acres). If it were farmed on the proprietor's own account, the cultivation, harvesting, threshing, and storing would amount to the value of 13,550 days' labour. The wages, seed, keep of horses and cattle, the interest of capital invested in stock, cost of superintendence, wear and tear of tools, etc., would stand him in 8,000 scudi, or 80 scudi per rubbio. The earth returns sevenfold on the seed sown. If 100 measures of seed are sown, the return will be 700. The average price of the measure of corn may be taken at 10 scudi. Thus the value of the crop will be 7,000 scudi, whereas the same crop cost to raise 8,000 scudi. Here are 1,000 scudi (about £215) flung clean into the gutter; and all for the pleasure of cultivating 100 rubbia of land. Is it not much better to let the 100 rubbia to a cattle-breeder, who will pay a rent of thirty or forty shillings per rubbio? On one side we have a clear loss of £215, and on the other a clear income of £160 or £184."

This reasoning is founded upon the calculations of Monsignore Nicolai, a prelate of considerable ability:† but it proves

* The rubbio is a measure both of land and of quantity.

† Monsignore Nicolai was a good practical agriculturist. He had a sort of model farm, known as the *Albereto Nicolai*, near the Basilica of St. Paul Without the Walls. He was an able administrator, and a man of superior attainments; and had he only possessed common honesty, he would have been in time a great man—as greatness is understood in Rome. He was a *Prelato di Fiochetto*, and held the post of *Uditore della R. C. Apostolica*, one of the four high offices which necessarily lead to Red Hats. Moreover, he was marked by Gregory XVI. for the promotion, and had actually ordered his scarlet apparel. But unfortunately Monsignore Nicolai affected the good things of this life over-much. He

nothing, because it attempts to prove too much. If the cul tivation of corn be really so ruinous an operation, it is strange that farmers should continue to grow it merely to spite the government.

But although it is quite true that the cultivation of a rubbio of land costs 80 scudi, it is false that the earth only yields sevenfold on the seed sown. According to the admission of the farmers themselves—and they are notoriously not in the habit of exaggerating their profits—it yields thirteenfold on the seed sown. Thirteen measures of corn are worth thirteen times ten scudi, or 130 scudi. Deduct 80, the cost of cultivation, and 50 remain. Multiply by 100, the result is 5,000 scudi (about £1,070), which will be the net income arising from the 100 rubbia cultivated in corn. The same extent of land under pasturage will produce £160 or £180.

was a *bon vivant*, and a *viveur*. He loved money, and he was utterly unscrupulous as to the means by which he obtained it. His career in the direction of the Sacred College was cut short, when he was very near its attainment, by a scandalous transaction, in which, although he was nearly eighty years of age, he played the principal part. He colluded with a notary, named Bachetti, to falsify the will of one Vitelli, a wealthy contractor, inserting in the place of the testator's two orphan nieces that of *his own natural son*. The affair having been dragged to light, Gregory XVI. deprived him of his office, and he ended his days in disgrace and retirement. His fondness for worldly pelf clung to him in his very last moments. A short time before he expired, he ordered some gendarmes to be brought into his bedroom, and charged them to watch over his property, lest anything should be stolen after he had ceased to breathe, and before the representatives of the law could take possession.

It is worthy of mention, as illustrating the administration of Justice in Rome, that even with these proofs of the invalidity of the will produced as that of Vitelli, his nieces were never able to recover the whole of his property. They were compelled to make terms with Grossi, the defunct Prelate's natural son, who to this day remains in the enjoyment of one-half of Vitelli's property!

Consider, moreover, that it is not the net, but the gross income, which constitutes the wealth of a country. The cultivation of 100 rubbia, before it puts 5,000 scudi into the farmer's pockets, has put some 8,000 scudi in circulation. These eight thousand scudi are distributed among a thousand or fifteen hundred poor creatures who are sadly in want of them. Pasture-farming, on the contrary, is only profitable to three persons, the landlord, the breeder, and the herdsman. Add to this, that in substituting arable for pasture farming, you substitute health for disease, a more important consideration than any other.

But churchmen who hold or administer lands in mortmain, will never consent to such a salutary resolution. It does not profit them directly enough. As long as they have the upper hand, they will prefer their own ease, and the certainty of their income, to the future welfare of the people.

Pius VI., a Pope worthy to have statues erected to him, conceived the heroic project of forcing a change upon them. He decided that 23,000 rubbia should be annually cultivated in the Agro Romano, and that all the land should in turn be subjected to manual labour. Pius VII. did still better. He decided that Rome, the *origo mali*, should be the first to apply the remedy. He had a circuit of a mile traced round the capital, and ordered the proprietors to cultivate it without further question. A second, and then a third, were to succeed to the first. The result would have been the disappearance, in a few years, of malaria, and the gradual population of the solitudes. The purification of the atmosphere would, too, be further promoted by planting trees round the fields. Excellent measures these, although tinged by despotism. Enlightened despotism repairs the errors of clumsy despotism. But what could the will of two men avail against the passive resistance of a caste? The laws of Pius

VI. and Pius VII. were never enforced. Cultivation, which had extended over 16,000 rubbia under the reign of Pius VI., is reduced to an annual average of 5,000 or 6,000 under the paternal inspection of Pius IX. Not only is the planting of young trees abandoned, but the sheep are allowed to nibble down the tender shoots of the old ones. Besides this, speculators are tolerated, who burn down whole forests, for the production of potash.

The estates of the Roman princes are somewhat better cultivated than those of the Church: but they are involved in the same movement, or, more strictly speaking, enchained in the same stagnation. The law, which retains immense domains for ever in the hands of the same family, and custom, which obliges the Roman nobles to spend so large a portion of their incomes upon show, are equally obstacles to the subdivision and to the improvement of the land.

And while the richest plains in Italy are thus lying dormant, a vigorous, indefatigable, and heroic population cultivates with the pickaxe the arid sides of mountains, and exhausts its strength in attempting to extract vegetation from flints.

I have described the small mountain proprietors who form the populations of the towns of 10,000 inhabitants towards the Mediterranean. You have seen with what indomitable resolution they combat the sterility of their meagre domains, without any hope of ever becoming rich. These poor people, who spend their lives in getting their living, would fancy themselves transported to Paradise, if anybody were to give them a long lease of half-a-dozen acres in the country about Rome. Their labour would then have a purpose, their existence an aim, their family a future.

Perhaps you think they would refuse to labour in an unhealthy country. Why, these are the very men who at present cultivate the Roman Campagna to such extent as it is allowed to be cultivated. They it is who, every spring, come down in large companies from their native mountains, to break up the heavy clods with pickaxes, and complete the work of the plough. It is they, too, who return to harvest the crop under the fatal heat of the summer sun. They attack a field waving with golden corn. They reap from dawn to dusk, with no food more nourishing than bread and cheese. They sleep in the open field, regardless of the nocturnal exhalations which float around them—and some of them never rise again. Those who survive ten days of a harvest more destructive than many a battle, return to their native village with some four or five scudi in their pockets.

If these men could obtain a long lease, or merely take the land from year to year, they would make more money, and the dangers to be encountered would be no greater. They might be established between Rome and Montepoli, Rome and Civita Castellana, in the valley of Ceprano, on the hills extending round the *Castelli* of Rome, where they would breathe an air as wholesome as that of their own mountains; for fever does not always spare them even there. In course of time, the colonizing system, advancing slowly and gradually, might realize the dream of Pius VII., and would inevitably drive before it pauperism and disease.

I dare not hope that such a miracle will ever be wrought by a Pope. The resistance to be encountered is too great, and the power is too inert. But if it should ever please Heaven, which has given them ten centuries of clerical government, to accord them, by way of compensation, ten blessed years of lay administration, we should perhaps see the Church property placed in more active and abler hands.

Then, too, we should see the law of primogeniture and the system of entails abolished, large estates divided, and their owners reduced, by the force of circumstances, to the necessity of cultivating their properties. Good laws on exportation, well enforced, would enable spirited farmers to cultivate corn on a large scale. A network of country roads, and main lines of railway, would convey agricultural produce from one end of the country to the other. A national fleet would carry it all over the world. Public works, institutions of credit, police— But why plunge into such a sea of hopes?

Suffice it to say, that the subjects of the Pope will be as prosperous and as happy as any people in Europe—as soon as they cease to be governed by a Pope!

CHAPTER XX.

FINANCES.

"The subjects of the Pope are necessarily poor—but then they pay hardly any taxes. The one condition is a compensation for the other!"

This is what both you and I have often heard said. Now and then, too, it is put forth upon the faith of some statistical return or another of the Golden Age, that they are governed at the rate of 7*s.* 6*d.* per head.

This calculation is a mere fable, as I can easily prove. But supposing it to be correct, the Romans would not be the less deserving of pity. It is a miserable consolation to people who have nothing, to be told that their taxes are low. For my part, I would much rather have heavy taxes to pay, and a good deal to pay them with, like the English. What would be thought of the Queen's government, if after having ruined trade, manufactures, and agriculture, and exhausted all the sources of public prosperity, it were to say to the people, "Rejoice, good people, for henceforth your taxes will not exceed 7*s.* 6*d.* a head all round!" The English people would answer with great reason, that they would much prefer to pay £40 a head, and be able to make £400.

It is not this or that particular sum per head on a population which constitutes moderate or excessive taxation; but the relation which the sum annually taken for the service of the State bears to the revenues of the nation. It is just to take much from him who has much; monstrous to attempt to take anything—be it never so little—from him who has nothing. If you examine the question from this common sense point of view, you will agree with me that taxation at the rate of 7*s.* 6*d.* a head, is pretty heavy for the poor Romans.

But 7*s.* 6*d.* a head is *not* the rate at which they are taxed; nor even double that amount. The Budget of Rome is £2,800,000, which is to be assessed upon three million taxpayers.

Assessed, moreover, not according to the laws of reason, justice, and humanity, but in such a manner that the heaviest burdens fall upon the most useful, laborious, and interesting class of the nation, the small proprietors.

And I do not allude here to the taxes paid directly to the State, and admitted in the budget. Besides these, there are the provincial and municipal charges, which, under the title of additional per-centage, amount to more than double the direct taxes. The province of Bologna pays £80,900 of property-tax, and £96,812 of provincial and municipal charges, making together £177,712. This sum distributed over the whole population of 370,107, brings the taxation to a fraction under 10*s.* a head. But observe, that instead of being borne by the whole population, it is borne by no more than 23,022 proprietors.

But mark a further injustice! It does not bear equally upon the proprietors of the towns and those of the country. The former has a great advantage over the latter. A town property in the province of Bologna pays 2*s.* 3*d.* per cent., a country property of the same value 5*s.* 3*d.* per cent., not upon the income, but the capital.

In the towns, it is not the palaces, but the houses of the

middle class that are the most heavily rated. Take the palace of a nobleman in Bologna, and a small house belonging to a citizen, which adjoins it. The palace is valued at the trifling sum of £1,100, on the ground that the apartments inhabited by the owner are not included in the income. The actual rent of which the owner is in the receipt for the part left off is about £280 a year: his taxes are £18 a year. The small house adjoining is valued at £200. The rent derived from it is £10 a year, and the taxes paid on it are £3. 7*s.* 6*d.* Thus we find the palace paying something like 5*s.* 6*d.* per cent. on its income, and the small house £1 7*s.*

The Lombards justly excite our compassion. But the proprietors of the province of Bologna are taxed to the annual amount of £1,400 more than those of the province of Milan.

To this crushing taxation are added heavy duties on articles of consumption. All the necessaries of life are liable to these taxes, such as flour, vegetables, rice, bread, etc. They are heavier than in almost any other European city. Meat is charged at the same rate as in Paris. Hay, straw, and wood, at still higher rates.

The town dues of Lille amount to 10*s.* per head on the population; those of Florence, about the same; and those of Lyons 12*s.* 6*d.* At Bologna they are 14*s.* 2*d.* Observe, town dues alone. We are already a long way from the 7*s.* 6*d.* of the Golden Age!

I am bound in justice to admit that the nation has not always been so hardly dealt with. It was not till the reign of Pius IX. that the taxation became insupportable. The budget of Bologna was more than doubled between 1846 and 1858.

Something might be said, if at least the money taken from the nation were spent for the good of the nation!

But one-third of the amount raised in taxation remains in the hands of the officials who collect it. This is incredible, but true. The cost of collecting the revenue amounts, if I mistake not, in England, to 8 per cent.; in France, to 14 per cent.; in Piedmont, to 16 per cent.; and in the States of the Church, to 31 per cent.

If you marvel at a system of extravagance which obliges the people to pay £4 for every £2. 15*s.* 10*d.* required for their mis-government, here is a fact which will enlighten you on the subject.

Last year the place of municipal receiver was put up to auction in the city of Bologna. An offer was made by an honourable and responsible man to collect the dues for a commission of 1½ per cent. The Government gave the preference to Count Cesare Mattei, one of the Pope's Chamberlains, who asked two per cent. So this piece of favouritism costs the city £800 a year.

The following is the mode in which the revenue (after the abstraction of one-third in the course of collecting it) is disposed of.

£1,000,000 goes to pay the interest of a continually accumulating debt, contracted by the priests, and for the priests, annually increasing through the bad administration of the priests, and carried by the priests to the debit of the nation.

£400,000 is devoured by a useless army, the sole duty of which has hitherto been to present arms to the Cardinals, and to escort the procession of the Host.

£120,000 is devoted to those establishments which of all others are the most indispensable to an unpopular government: I mean, the prisons.

£80,000 is the cost of the administration of justice. The tribunals of the capital absorb half the amount, because they enjoy the distinction of being for the most part composed of prelates.

The very modest sum of £100,000 is devoted to public works. This is chiefly spent in embellishing Rome, and repairing churches.

£60,000 goes in the encouragement of idleness in the city of Rome. A Charity Commission, presided over by a Cardinal, distributes this sum among a few thousand incorrigible idlers, without accounting for it to anybody. Mendicity is all the more flourishing, as is apparent to every one. From 1827 to 1858, the subjects of the Holy Father paid £1,600,000 in mischievous alms, among the injurious effects of which, the principal was to deprive labour of the hands it required. The Cardinal who presides over the Commission takes £2,400 a year for his private charities.

£16,000 defrays poorly enough the cost of the public education, which, moreover, is wholly in the hands of the clergy. Add this moderate sum, and the £80,000 devoted to the administration of justice, to a part of the £100,000 spent on public works, and you have all that can fairly be set down as money spent in the service of the nation. The remainder is of no use but to the Government,—in other words, to a parcel of priests.

The Pope and the partners of his power must be indifferent financiers, when, after spending such a pittance on the nation, they contrive to wind up every year with a deficit. The balance of 1858 showed a deficit of nearly half a million sterling, which does not prevent the government from promising a surplus in the estimates of 1859.

In order to fill up the gaps in the budget, the Government has recourse to borrowing, sometimes openly, by a loan from the house of Rothschild, sometimes secretly, by an issue of stock.

In 1857 the Pontifical Government contracted its eleventh loan with Rothschild's house; it was a trifle, something under £700,000. Nevertheless there were quiet issues of stock from 1851 to 1858, to the tune of £1,320,000.

The capital of the debt for which its subjects are liable, amounts to £14,376,150. 5*s.* If you will take the trouble to divide this grand total by the figure which represents the population, you will find that every little subject born to the Pope comes into the world a debtor of something like £4. 10*s.*, whereof he will contribute to pay the interest all his life, although neither he nor his ancestors have ever derived the least benefit from the outlay.

It is true these fourteen millions and a half (in round numbers) have not been lost for all the world. The nephews of the Popes have pocketed a good round sum. About a third has been swallowed up by what is called the general interests of the Roman Catholic faith. It has been proved that the religious wars have cost the Popes at least four millions; and the farmers of Ancona and Forlì are still paying out of the produce of their fields for the faggots used to burn the Huguenots. The churches of which Rome is so proud have not been paid for entirely by the tribute of Catholicism at large. There are certain remnants of accounts, which were at the cost of the Roman people. The Popes have made more than one donation to those poor religious establishments, which possess no more than £20,000,000 worth of property in the world. The expenses lumped together under the head of Allocations for Public Worship add something short of £900,000 sterling to the national debt. Foreign occupation, and more particularly the invasion of the Austrians in the north, has burdened the inhabitants with a million sterling. Add the money squandered, given away, stolen, and lost, together with £1,360,000 paid to bankers for commission on loans, and you have an account of the total of the debt, excepting perhaps a million and a half or so, of which the unexplained and inexplicable disbursement does immortal honour to the discretion of the ministers.

Since the restoration of Pius IX., an approach to respect for public opinion has forced the Pontifical Government to publish some sort of accounts. It does not render them to the nation, but to Europe, knowing that Europe is not curious in the matter, and will be easily satisfied. A few copies of the annual Budget are published; they are certainly not in everybody's reach. The statement of receipts and expenditure is prodigiously laconic. I have now before me the estimates prepared for 1858, in four pages, the least blank of which contains just fourteen lines. The Finance Minister sums up the receipts and the outgoings, both ordinary and extraordinary. Under the head of Receipts, he lumps the whole of "the direct contributions, and the State property, 3,201,426 scudi."

Under the head of Expenditure, we read "Commerce, Fine Arts, Agriculture, Manufactures, and Public Works, 601,764 scudi." A tolerable lump, this.

This powerful simplification of accounts enables the Minister to perform some capital tricks of financial sleight of hand. Supposing, for instance, the Government wants half a million of scudi for some mysterious purpose, nothing is easier than to bring their direct contributions in as having paid half a million less than they really have. What will Europe ever know about the matter?

"Speech is silver, but silence is gold."

Successive Finance Ministers at Rome have all adopted this device, even when they are forced to speak, they have the art of not saying the very thing the country wants to hear.

In almost all civilized countries the nation enjoys two rights which seem perfectly just and natural. The first is that of voting the taxes, either directly or through the medium of its deputies; the second, that of verifying the expenditure of its own money.

In the Papal kingdom, the Pope or his Minister says to the citizens, "Here is what you have to pay!" And he takes the money, spends it, and never more alludes to it except in the vaguest language.

Still, in order to afford some sort of satisfaction to the conscience of Europe, Pius IX. promised to place the finances under the control of a sort of Chamber of Deputies. Here is the text of this promise, which figured, with many others, in the *Motu Proprio* of the 12th of September, 1849.

"*A Consulta di Stato* for the Finances is established. It will be *heard* on the estimates of the forthcoming year. It will examine the balance of accounts for the previous year, and sign the vote of credit. It will give its advice on the establishment of new, or the reduction of old taxes; on the better distribution of the general taxation; on the measures to be taken for the improvement of commerce, and in general on all that concerns the interests of the public Treasury.

"The Councillors shall be selected by Us from lists presented by the Provincial Councils. Their number shall be fixed in proportion to the provinces of the State. This number may be increased within fixed limits by the addition of some of our subjects, whom we reserve to ourselves the right to name."

Now, allow me to dwell briefly upon the meaning of this promise, and the results which have followed it. Who knows whether diplomacy may not ere long be again occupied in demanding promises of the Pope ?—whether the Pope may not again think it wise to promise mountains and marvels ? —whether these new promises may not be just as hollow and insincere as the old ones ? This short paragraph deserves a long commentary, for it is fraught with instruction.

" It is established ! " said the Pope. But the *Consulta di Stato* of Finances, established the 12th of September, 1849, only gave signs of life in December, 1853. Four years afterwards ! This is what I call drawing a bill at a pretty long date. It is admitted that the nation needs some guarantees, and that it is entitled to tender some advice, and to exercise some control. And so the nation is requested to call again in four years.

The members of the *Consulta* of the Finances are a sort of sham deputies; very sham ones, I assure you, although the Count de Rayneval, to suit his purpose, is pleased to call them "the Representatives of the Nation." They represent the nation as Cardinal Antonelli represents the Apostles.

They are elected by the Pope from a list presented by the Communal Councils. The Communal Councillors are elected by their predecessors of the Communal Council, who were chosen directly by the Pope from a list of eligible citizens, each of whom must have produced a certificate of good conduct, both religious and political. In all this I cannot for the life of me see more than one elector—the Pope.

We'll begin this progressive election again, and start from the very bottom—that is, the nation. The Italians have a peculiar fancy for municipal liberties. The Pope knows this, and, as a good prince, he resolves to accommodate them. The township or commune wishes to choose its own councillors, of which there are ten to be elected. The Pope names sixty electors—six electors for every councillor. And observe, that in order to become an elector, a certificate from the parish and the police is necessary. But they are not infallible; and, moreover, it is just possible that in the exercise of a novel right they may fall into some error; so the Sovereign determines to arrange the election himself. Then, his Communal Councillors—for they are indeed *his*—come and present him with a list of candidates for the Provincial Council. The list is long, in order that the Holy Father may have scope for his selection. For instance, in the province of Bologna he chooses eleven names out of one hundred and fifty-six; he must be unlucky indeed not to be able to pick out eleven men devoted to him. These eleven Provincial Councillors, in their turn, present four candidates, out of whom the Pope chooses one. And this is how the nation is *represented* in the Financial Council.

Still, with a certain luxury of suspicion, the Holy Father adds to the list of representatives some men of his own choice, his own caste, and who are in habits of intimacy with him. The councillors elected by the nation are eliminated by one-third every two years. The councillors named directly by the Pope are irremovable.

Verily, if ever constituted body offered guarantees to power, it was this Council of Finances. And yet, the Pope does not trust to it. He has given the presidence to a Cardinal, the vice-presidence to a Prelate; and still he is only half re-assured. A special regulation places all the councillors under the supreme control of the Cardinal President. It is he who names the commissioners, organizes the bureaux, and makes the reports to the Pope. Without his permission no papers or documents are communicated to the councillors. So true is it that the reigning caste sees in every layman an enemy.

And the reigning caste is quite right. These poor lay councillors, selected among the most timid, submissive, and devoted of the Pope's subjects, could not forget that they were men, citizens, and Italians. On the day after their installation they manifested a desire to begin doing their duty, by examining the accounts of the preceding year. They were told that these accounts were lost. They persisted in their demands. A search was instituted. A few documents were produced; but so incomplete that the Council was not able in six years to audit and pass them.

The advice of the Council of Finances was not taken on the new taxes decreed between 1849 and 1853. Since 1853, that is to say, since the Council of Finances has entered upon its functions, the Government has contracted foreign loans, inscribed consolidated stock in the great book of the national debt, alienated the national property, signed postal conventions, changed the system of taxation at Benevento, and taxed the diseased vines, without even taking the trouble to ascertain its opinion.

The Government proposed some other financial measure to the Council, and the answer was in the negative. In spite of this, the Government measures were carried into execution. The *Motu Proprio* says the *Consulta di Stato* shall be heard, but not that it shall be listened to.*

Every year, at the end of the session, the *Consulta* addresses to the Pope a humble petition against the gross abuses of the financial system. The Pope remits the petition

* All the facts and figures contained in this chapter are taken from the works of the Marchese Pepoli.

over to some Cardinals. The Cardinals remit it over to the Greek Kalends.

The Count de Rayneval greatly admired this mechanism. The Emperor Soulouque did more—he imitated it.

But M. Guizot tells us that "there is a degree of bad government which no people, whether great or little, enlightened or ignorant, will tolerate at the present day."*

* Memoirs, vol. ii. p. 293.

CONCLUSION.

The Count de Rayneval, after having proved that all is for the best in the dominions of the Pope, winds up his celebrated Note by a desponding conclusion. According to him, the Roman Question is one which cannot possibly be definitively solved; and the utmost that can be effected by diplomacy is the postponement of a catastrophe.

I am not such a pessimist. It appears to me that all political questions may be solved, and all catastrophes averted. I am sanguine enough to believe that war is not absolutely indispensable to the salvation of Italy and the security of Europe, and that it is possible to extinguish a conflagration without firing guns.

You have seen the intolerable misery and the legitimate discontent of the subjects of the Pope. You know enough of them to understand that Europe ought without delay to bring them succour, not only from the love of abstract justice, but in the interest of the public peace. I have proved to you that the misfortunes which afflict these three millions of men must be attributed neither to the weakness of the sovereign, nor even to the perversity of minister, but are the logical and necessary deductions from a principle. All that Europe has to do is to protest against the consequences. The principle must either be admitted or rejected. If you approve the temporal sovereignty of the Pope, you are bound to applaud everything, even the conduct of Cardinal Antonelli. If you are shocked by the offences of the Pontifical Government, it is against the ecclesiastical monarchy that you must seek your remedy.

Diplomacy, without staying to discuss the premises, has from time to time protested against the deductions. In profoundly respectful *Memoranda* it has implored the Pope to act inconsistently, by administering the affairs of his States upon the principles of lay governments. Should the Pope turn a deaf ear, the diplomatists have no right to complain, because they recognize his character, as an independent sovereign. Should he promise all they ask and afterwards break his word, diplomacy is equally without a ground of complaint. Is it not the admitted right of the Sovereign Pontiff to absolve men even from the most solemn oaths? And finally, should he yield to the solicitation of Europe, and enact liberal laws one day, only to let them fall into desuetude the next, diplomatists are once more disarmed. To violate its own laws is a special privilege of absolute monarchy.

I entertain a very high respect for our diplomatists of 1859; nor were their predecessors of 1831 wanting either in good intentions or capacity. They addressed to Gregory XVI. a MEMORANDUM, which is a master-piece of its kind. They extorted from the Pope a real constitution,—a constitution which left nothing to be desired, and which guaranteed all the moral and material interests of the Roman nation. In a few years this same constitution had entirely disappeared, and abuses again flowed from the ecclesiastical principle, like a river from its source.

We renewed the experiment in 1849. The Pope granted us the *Motu Proprio* of Portici, and the Romans gained nothing by it.

Shall our diplomatists repeat in 1859 this same part of dupes? A French engineer has demonstrated that dykes erected along the banks of rivers liable to inundation are costly, in constant need of repair, and ineffectual; and that the only real protection against those devastations is the construction of a dam at the source. To the source, then, gentlemen of the diplomatic guild! Ascend straight to the temporal power of the Papacy.

And yet I dare neither hope for, nor ask of Europe the immediate application of this grand panacea. Gerontocracy is still too powerful, even in the youngest governments Besides, we are now at peace, and radical reforms are only to be effected by war. The sword alone enjoys the privilege of deciding great questions by a single stroke. Diplomatists, a timid army of peace, proceed but by half-measures.

There is one which was proposed in 1814 by Count Aldini, in 1831 by Rossi, in 1855 by Count Cavour. These three statesmen, comprehending the impossibility of limiting the authority of the Pope within the kingdom in which it is exercised, and over the people who are abandoned to it, advised Europe to remedy the evil by diminishing the extent of, and reducing the population subjected to, the States of the Church.

Nothing is more just, natural, or easy than to free the Adriatic provinces, and to confine the despotism of the Papacy between the Mediterranean and the Apennines. I have shown that the cities of Ferrara, Ravenna, Bologna, Rimini, and Ancona are at once the most impatient of the Pontifical yoke and the most worthy of liberty. Deliver them. Here is a miracle which may be wrought by a stroke of the pen: and the eagle's plume which signed the treaty of Paris is as yet but freshly mended.

There would still remain to the Pope a million of subjects, and between three and four millions of acres; neither the one nor the other in a very high state of cultivation, I must admit; but it is possible that the diminution of his revenue might induce him to manage his estates and utilize his resources better than he now does. One of two things would occur: either he would enter upon the course pursued by good governments, and the condition of his subjects would become endurable, or he would persist in the errors of his predecessors, and the Mediterranean provinces would in their turn demand their independence.

At the worst, and as a last alternative, the Pope might retain the city of Rome, his palaces and temples, his cardinals and prelates, his priests and monks, his princes and footmen, and Europe would contribute to feed the little colony.

Rome, surrounded by the respect of the universe, as by a Chinese wall, would be, so to speak, a foreign body in the midst of free and living Italy. The country would suffer neither more nor less than does an old soldier from the bullet which the surgeon has left in his leg.

But will the Pope and the Cardinals easily resign themselves to the condition of mere ministers of religion? Will they willingly renounce their political influence? Will they in a single day forget their habits of interfering in our affairs, of arming princes against one another, and of discreetly stirring up citizens against their rulers? I much doubt it.

But on the other hand, princes will avail themselves of the lawful right of self-defence. They will read history, and they will there find that the really strong governments are those which have kept religious authority in their own hands; that the Senate of Rome did not grant the priests of Carthage liberty to preach in Italy; that the Queen of England and the Emperor of Russia are the heads of the Anglican and Russian religions; and they will see that by right the sovereign metropolis of the churches of France should be in Paris.

THE END.

Meta Gray; or, What Makes Home Happy. By MARIA J. McINTOSH, Author of "Aunt Kitty's Tales." 1 vol., 12mo. 75 cents.

The Emancipation of Faith. By the late HENRY EDWARD SCHEDEL, M. D. Edited by GEORGE SCHEDEL. 2 vols. 8vo. Cloth, $4

The Ministry of Life. By MARIA LOUISA CHARLESWORTH, Author of "Ministering Children.
1 volume, 12mo. Cloth, with 2 engravings, $1

Bertram Noel: A Story of Youth. By E. J. MAY, Author of "Edgar Clifton." 1 volume, 16mo. Illustrated, 75 cents.

Benton's Thirty Years' View; or, A History of the Working of the American Government for Thirty Years, from 1820 to 1850. New edition, with Autobiography and a General Index. 2 volumes, 8vo. Cloth, $5.

The Household Book of Poetry. Collected and Edited by CHARLES A. DANA. Third Edition. 1 volume, half morocco, $3 50.

New York to Delhi, by the way of Rio de Janeiro, Australia, and China. By ROBERT B. MINTURN, JR.
1 volume, 12mo. Illustrated with a Map, $1 25. (Second edt.)

History of Civilization in England. By HENRY THOMAS BUCKLE. Vol. 1, 8vo. 677 pages. From the 2d London edt., $2 50.

Rational Cosmology; or, The Eternal Principles and the Necessary Laws of the Universe. By LAURENS P. HICKOK, D. D. 1 volume, 8vo. 397 pages, $1 75.

Whewell's History of the Inductive Sciences. First American, from the third London edition. 2 vols, 8vo. Cloth, $4.

The Coopers; or, Getting Under Way. By ALICE B HAVEN. 1 volume, 12mo. 336 page, 75 cents

Appleton's New American Cyclopædia. A Popular Dictionary of General Knowledge. Volume V. Just published. To be completed in fifteen volumes.
Cloth, $3; leather, $3 50; hf. mor. $4; hf. Russia, $4 50. Published by subscription.

Benton's Abridgment of the Congressional Debates. Volume X. Just published. Sold by Subscription.
Cloth, $3; law sheep, $3 50; half morocco, $4. Each volume payable as delivered.

Burton's Cyclopædia of Wit and Humor. Two large volumes, 8vo. Profusely illustrated with Wood Engravings and twenty-four Portraits on Steel.
Extra cloth, $7; sheep extra, $8; hf mor. $9; hf calf, $10

The Banks of New York; Their Dealers; The Clearing-House; and the Panic of 1857. With a Financial Chart. By J. S. Gibbons. With Thirty Illustrations, by Herrick. 1 vol. 12mo. 400 pages. Cloth, $1.50.

A book for every Man of Business, for the Bank Officer and Clerk; for the Bank Stockholder and Depositor; and especially for the Merchant and his Cash Manager; also for the Lawyer, who will here find the exact Responsibilities that exist between the different officers of Banks and the Clerks, and between them and the Dealers.

The operations of the Clearing-House are described in detail, and illustrated by a financial Chart, which exhibits, in an interesting manner, the Fluctuations of the Bank Loans.

The immediate and exact cause of the Panic of 1857 *is clearly demonstrated by the records of the Clearing-House, and a scale is presented by which the deviation of the volume of Bank Loans from an average standard of safety can be ascertained at a single glance.*

History of the State of Rhode Island and Providence Plantations. By Samuel Greene Arnold. Vol. I. 1636 -1700. 1 vol. 8vo. 574 pages. $2.50.

To trace the rise and progress of a State, the offspring of ideas that were novel and startling, even amid the philosophical speculations of the Seventeenth Century; whose birth was a protest against, whose infancy was a struggle with, and whose maturity was a triumph over, the retrograde tendency of established Puritanism; a State that was the second-born of persecution, whose founders had been doubly tried in the purifying fire; a State which, more than any other, has exerted, by the weight of its example, an influence to shape the political ideas of the present day, whose moral power has been in the inverse ratio with its material importance; of which an eminent Historian of the United States has said that, had its territory "corresponded to the importance and singularity of the principles of its early existence, the world would have been filled with wonder at the phenomena of its history," is a task not to be lightly attempted or hastily performed."—Extract from Preface.

The Ministry of Life. By Maria Louisa Charlesworth, Author of "Ministering Children." 1 vol., 12mo., with Two Eng's., $1. Of the "Ministering Children," (the author's previous work,) 50,000 copies have been sold.

"*The higher walks of life, the blessedness of doing good, and the paths of usefulness and enjoyment, are drawn out with beautiful simplicity, and made attractive and easy in the attractive pages of this author. To do good, to teach others how to do good, to render the home circle and the neighborhood glad with the voice and hand of Christian charity, is the aim of the author, who has great power of description, a genuine love for evangelical religion, and blends instruction with the story, so as to give charm to all her books.*"—N. Y. Observer.

The Coopers; or, Getting Under Way. By ALICE B HAVEN, Author of "No Such Word as Fail," "All's Not Gold that Glitters," etc., etc. 1 vol. 12mo. 336 pages. 75 cents.

"To grace and freshness of style, Mrs. Haven adds a genial, cheerful philosophy of Life, and Naturalness of Character and Incident, in the History of the Cooper Family.

A Text Book of Vegetable and Animal Physiology. Designed for the use of Schools, Seminaries and Colleges in the United States. By HENRY GOADBY, M. D., Professor of Vegetable and Animal Physiology and Entomology, in the State Agricultural College of Michigan, &c. A new edition. One handsome vol., 8vo., embellished with upwards of 450 wood engravings (many of them colored,) Price, $2

"The attempt to teach only Human Physiology, like a similar proceeding in regard to Anatomy, can only end in failure; whereas, if the origin (so to speak) of the organic structures in the animal kingdom, be sought for and steadily pursued through all the classes, showing their gradual complication, and the necessity for the addition of accessory organs, till they reach their utmost development and culminate in man, the study may be rendered an agreeable and interesting one, and be fruitful in profitable results.

"Throughout the accompanying pages, this principle has been kept steadily in view, and it has been deemed of more importance to impart solid and thorough instruction on the subjects discussed, rather than embrace the whole field of physiology, and, for want of space, fail to do justice to any part of it."—EXTRACT FROM PREFACE.

The Physiology of Common Life. By GEORGE HENRY LEWES, Author of "Seaside Studies," "Life of Goethe," etc. No. 1. Just Ready. Price 10 cents.

EXTRACT FROM PROSPECTUS.

No scientific subject can be so important to Man as that of his own Life. No knowledge can be so incessantly appealed to by the incidents of every day, as the knowledge of the processes by which he lives and acts. At every moment he is in danger of disobeying laws which, when disobeyed, may bring years of suffering, decline of powers, premature decay. Sanitary reformers preach in vain, because they preach to a public which does not understand the laws of life—laws as rigorous as those of Gravitation or Motion. Even the sad experience of others yields us no lessons, unless we understand the principles involved. If one Man is seen to suffer from vitiated air, another is seen to endure it without apparent harm; a third concludes that "it is all chance," and trusts to that chance. Had he understood the principle involved, he would not have been left to chance—his first lesson in swimming would not have been a shipwreck.

The work will be illustrated with from 20 to 25 woodcuts, to assist the exposition. It will be published in monthly numbers, uniform with Johnston's "Chemistry of Common Life."

The History of Civilization in England. By HENRY THOS. BUCKLE. Vol. I. 8vo. Cloth. $2.50

Whoever misses reading this book, will miss reading what is, in various respects, to the best of our judgment and experience, the most remarkable book of the day—one, indeed, that no thoughtful, inquiring mind would miss reading for a good deal. Let the reader be as adverse as he may to the writer's philosophy, let him be as devoted to the obstructive as Mr. Buckle is to the progress party, let him be as orthodox in church creed as the other is heterodox, as dogmatic as his author is sceptical,—let him, in short, find his prejudices shocked at every turn of the argument, and all his prepossessions whistled down the wind,—still, there is so much in this extraordinary volume to stimulate reflection, and excite to inquiry, and provoke to earnest investigation, perhaps (to this or that reader) on a track hitherto untrodden, and across the virgin soil of untilled fields, fresh woods and pastures new,—that we may fairly defy the most hostile spirit, the most mistrustful and least sympathetic, to read it through without being glad of having done so, or, having begun it, or even glanced at almost any one of its 854 pages, to pass it away unread.—NEW MONTHLY (LONDON) MAGAZINE.

Legends and Lyrics. By ANNE ADELAIDE PROCTOR, (Daughter of the Poet, Barry Cornwall.) One very neat volume, 12mo. Second edition. 75 cents.

This is the charming volume of fresh and tender poems, by the daughter of one of England's most honored and popular poets, which has lately been received with so hearty a welcome in England and America. Choice portions of it, copied by the press with lively praises, have found their way to the firesides.

The Household Book of Poetry. Collected and Edited by CHARLES A. DANA. 1 vol. 8vo. 793 pages. Third edition. In half morocco. Gilt top. $3.50.

As the New-York correspondent of The Boston Transcript enthusiastically writes, 'The elegiac composition, the exquisite sonnet, the genuine pastoral, the war-song and rural hymn, whose cadences are as remembered music, and the couplets whose chime rings out from the depths of the heart; whatever the old English dramatists, the ode writers of the reign of Anne and Charles, the purest disciples of heroic verse, the Lakists, the Byronic school—Wordsworth and Dryden, Mrs. Hemans and Scott, Shakspeare and Hartley Coleridge have made precious to soul and sense, are herein brought together; and more than this—the many isolated single notes, whose lingering harmony embalms their author's name, with the numerous fugitive "brilliants," heretofore of unknown parentage, cut from newspapers for the last half century—the deep, soulfull utterances of heroes and mourners, lovers and exiles, devotees of nature and worshippers of art—are here elegantly garnered and chronicled.'

"It is just such a volume as a man may give to a woman, albeit that woman is his mother, his sister, or his wife, and is richly worth the place it claims on a lower shelf within arm's length, in the most select library."—CHICAGO JOURNAL.

The Handy-Book on Property Law, in a series of Letters. By Lord St. Leonards, (Sir Edward Sugden.) 1 vol., 16mo., Cloth, 75 cents.

"This excellent little work gives the plainest instructions in all matters connected with selling, buying, mortgaging, leasing, settling and devising estates; and informs us of our relations to our properties, our wives, our children, and our liabilities as trustees, executors, &c., &c."—TRIBUNE.

The Manual of Chess; Containing the Elementary Principles of the Game. Illustrated with numerous Diagrams, recent Games and Original Problems. By CHARLES KENNY. 1 vol. 12mo. Price 50 cents.

"Within the compass of this work I have included all that is necessary for the beginner to learn. In recommendation of this Manual, I can safely assert that it contains more than any publication of the same dimensions. The Problems contained herein, as also one of the 'Games actually played,' are original, and have never been published.

The Book of Chess; Containing the Rudiments of the Game, and Elementary Analysis of the most Popular Openings, exemplified in games actually played by the great masters, including Staunton's Analysis of the Kings and Queens, Gambits, numerous Positions and Problems on Diagrams, both original and selected; also, a series of Chess Tales, with illustrations from original designs. The whole extracted and translated from the best sources. New Edition. By H. R. Agnel. $1.25.

Sixty Years' Gleanings from Life's Harvest. A Genuine Autobiography. By JOHN BROWN. 1 vol. 12mo. Cloth, $1.

"A remarkable book in every respect, and curiously interesting from beginning to end. John Brown lived with 'all his might,' and the 'Life' he writes is, in its abundance and variety of tragic and comic ups-and-downs, as good as a play. His experiences partook of all the quick changes and boisterous bustle, and rude humor of an old English fair; and as they are presented in this volume they afford a picture of the times he lived and incessantly moved in, which, in much of its bold handling, is not to be surpassed by less spirited pencils than those of Fielding and De Foe. The moral, even as you trace it through the bustling table of contents, is of unmistakable application for every fine young fellow of sound natural principles who has to shoulder his own way to good citizenship and a share of social influence.

"As a neglected child, a 'juvenile offender,' an ingenious vagabond, a shoemaker, a soldier, an actor, a sailor, a publican, a billiard-room keeper, a Town Councillor, and an author, Mr. Brown has seen the world for sixty years, and he unhesitatingly describes all that he has seen, with fidelity of memory and straightforward simplicity of style."

www.ingramcontent.com/pod-product-compliance
Lightning Source LLC
LaVergne TN
LVHW050529100826
845148LV00002B/492

* 9 7 8 1 4 2 5 5 1 9 3 4 6 *